T. B. (Thomas Beatty) Stewart

The coming conflict

A plea for prohibition

T. B. (Thomas Beatty) Stewart

The coming conflict
A plea for prohibition

ISBN/EAN: 9783742898104

Manufactured in Europe, USA, Canada, Australia, Japa

Cover: Foto ©Thomas Meinert / pixelio.de

Manufactured and distributed by brebook publishing software
(www.brebook.com)

T. B. (Thomas Beatty) Stewart

The coming conflict

THE

COMING CONFLICT

OR,

A PLEA FOR PROHIBITION.

—BY—

T. B. STEWART.

SAN FRANCISCO:

JOS. WINTERBURN & CO., BOOK AND JOB PRINTERS AND ELECTROTYPERS.

1887.

CONTENTS.

PREFACE.

THIS "Great Temperance Movement," which is des-
tined, ultimately, to sweep every "Grog-shop"
from the face of the Earth, had its birth in this
Country. Here, already, it has achieved its greatest tri-
umphs; and here, I believe, at no distant day, the arrogant
and accursed Liquor-Traffic will receive its death-blow.

Canada may possibly (?) have prohibition before we do;
but I feel confident that ours will be the first great Nation
of the World to prohibit the Importation, Manufacture and
Sale of all Intoxicating Liquors, to be used as a beverage.
England's noble example had much to do in leading us to
abolish Slavery, and other Nations have taught us many
precious lessons. May we not in some measure repay them
by teaching them the utter folly of continually bowing the
neck beneath the cruel yoke of Rum? While, as an Amer-
ican citizen, I would be delighted to see mine own Native
Land God's chosen Leader in this the greatest National
Reform the World has ever seen as yet; nevertheless, if it is
God's will that any other nation should gain this goal before
we do, I for one am ready to say "PRAISE THE LORD."

I regard the "Prohibition Movement" as one of the
grandest "Missionary Enterprises" of the ages. And while
I was studying the great Problem of the "Evangelization
of the World," two startling facts confronted me: 1. That
while we spend EIGHT MILLIONS for "Foreign Missions," we
are wasting THOUSANDS OF MILLIONS for Rum; and, 2, that
so-called CHRISTIAN NATIONS are sweeping vast hosts of the
heathen into the Drunkard's Hell. These facts led me to
write this little work. It has been written at odd moments
during the past five years, in the midst of my Theological
studies and Pastoral duties, and is necessarily very crude
and imperfect.

I lay no claim to the honored name "Poet," but have put my thoughts in this form, thinking they might be more widely read — although I know full well that "Didactic Poems" are very seldom a success. Still, the people are intensely interested in my THEME, and this, I trust, will make my work an exception, in spite of its many imperfections.

My Southern Brethren may think that I have made too much of the "Slavery Question," and that, like all Northerners, I am prejudiced against the South. Oh! No! my Southern Brother and Sister. I believe—just as you now do—that slavery was wrong, and that it was settled right, and it is only because the two great Reforms are alike in so many important respects, and so fresh in our memories, that I have referred to our recent conflict so often. But there is this vast difference: You of the Sunny South are rapidly melting away the coldness of the Conservative North, for you are *leading us* in this grand Prohibition fight, and God is using your noble enthusiasm for His cause, as the hammer to smite from the hands of the rum-cursed North, the hell-wrought shackles of the Demon Drink. I for one rejoice in the prosperity of the Southland, and am ready to meet all Southern Temperance Warriors on the grand battle-field of THE HOME AGAINST THE SALOON, and, standing over the grave of the old dead issues of the war, we will bury forever more the hatchet of fraternal strife "a hundred fathoms deep" God grant that Prohibition may wipe out these old sectional lines, and make our North and South, our East and West, a "Union now and forever, one and inseparable."

Many will differ from the views of this work, and some will criticise it harshly; but if my blessed Master, "whose I am and whom I serve," shall only be pleased to use this effort in the least degree, to hasten the coming of that happy time "when there shall be a Church and a School-house on every hill-top, and no saloon in the valley," I shall feel that my labor has not been "in vain in the Lord."

Certain of the triumph of the Truth in the Coming Conflict, I am yours for "God and Home and Humanity."

T. B. S.

DEDICATION.

To Him, my Savior, God and King,
Who gave, I trust, these thoughts I bring,
Concerning this momentous thing,
Of which my soul has tried to sing;

And next, to that true, Christian wife,
Who daily, in this deadly strife
Which puts the Liquor-Traffic to the knife
Has been the gentle cheerer of my life;

And to that noble Mother, grand,
Who early taught me, I should stand
For " God and Home and Native Land "
And fight their foes, on every hand;

And to those fearless men of might,
Who lead our forces in this fight,
Against Strong-Drink's accursed blight,
For Prohibition and the Right;

And to those noble, brave and fair,
Those Christian women, whose great care,
Is to uproot, by faith and prayer,
Drink's deadly Upas, everywhere;

And lastly, to God's holy Cause,—
Which seeks, by Prohibition laws,
To snatch all Nations from the jaws,
Of that vile Demon Drink, which draws

So many millions of our race,
Down to that horrid, awful place,
Which lies beneath God's angry face,
Unreached for ever by His grace:—

To these, I hereby dedicate,
The " COMING CONFLICT," and will wait
And hope—whatever be its fate,—
God's blessed Truth may penetrate

The minds of all; and that ere long,
Earth's rapidly-increasing throng,
Forever freed from Strong-Drink's wrong,
With happy voices, clear and strong,
Shall sing God's Prohibition song.

                    So prays,

                              THE AUTHOR.

PART I.

THE EVIL.

"Strong drink is raging."—Proverbs xx: 1.

I.

God spake the word, and into being sprang
This mighty nation of United States:
He laid our firm foundations, deep and broad,
And crowned our Country with abounding good.
Thus planted by His hand, within the midst
Of boundless blessings, in this Western World,
Our free **Republic** has from infancy
To sturdy manhood grown, until to-day,
It stands, confessed by all, a worthy peer
Of any kingdom Earth has ever known.

One hundred years and more, with grand success,
We have contended zealously against
The mighty evils, which from time to time
Have threatened to destroy, and sweep away
The well-built basis of our Union's life.

One such an evil was vile **Slavery,**
But did our nation sink beneath the weight
Of this enormous sin? Ah, No! She rose
And struck the dreadful shackles from the hands
Of unpaid toil; although it cost her much
Of gold, and of her best, her bravest blood.

6

That war-cloud's past, and as it fades away,
Upon its bosom rests the bow of Peace:
For now, instead of list'ning to the din
Of battle, and the tramp of warring hosts,
We hear the merry hum of busy wheels,
Or listen to the happy farmer's song,
Or watch the smoke from forge and furnace rise.

But is it all smooth sailing everywhere?
Are there no evils pressing on us now?
Oh, would 'twas so—but such is not the case.
Throughout the length and breadth of this fair land,
From every nook and corner, day by day,
A wail of woe on High ascends.   And why?
There is an evil, great and National,
To which both President and people, yea,
And statesmen, too, seem bound to shut their eyes;
And yet this sin is sapping secretly,
The very corner-stones, on which are built,
Our liberties and Institutions free.

We call this crime and curse Intemperance!
And is it not a greater curse to-day
By far, than ever was foul slavery.
For Slavery was local; but, alas!
Strong Drink holds almost universal sway.
The former bound the body, *not the soul;*
The latter *dooms them both* to endless death.

This giant evil, from our nation's birth,
Has slowly, but alas! most surely grown,
Until it is to-day, beyond all doubt,
The greatest moneyed power in the land.
Why, Manufacturing Monopolies,
And Railroad Companies, rich though they be,
Are, as to wealth, mere pigmies, when compared
With all the millions of the Liquor League.

In fact, no man on earth knows or can know
Exactly how much money, as a land,
We have invested in this monstrous trade.

Let any one go through our larger towns
And cities, yes, and even villages,
And count the groceries, hotels, saloons,
Vile dives, with all our dram-shop drug stores, too,
Where liquor in its varied forms is sold,
Both legally and in the face of law—
Let him go round and carefully inspect
Those massive buildings which he sees
Erected everywhere, throughout our land,
Where these intoxicants are made or stored—
Or let him visit those palatial homes
Where Liquor Dealers dwell, or seat himself
Beside them in their royal carriages,
As through our streets they roll, in grandest style,
Their persons decked in broadcloth, satins, silks,
And, flashing over all, resplendent gems
And costly jewels, fit for crowns of kings—
Then let him tell us, if he thinks he can, (?)
How many countless millions of our wealth
We have invested in this awful trade! (?)

No wonder Temp'rance workers are dismayed,
And in their anguish, lifting up their voice
They cry: How long, O Lord! how long? HOW LONG?

II.

But what effect does this vast trade produce
Upon the Commonwealth at large? 'tis asked.
Is it a blessing to us, or a curse?
THIS IS THE GREATEST QUESTION OF THE AGE,
WITHOUT A DOUBT. How shall we answer it?

By ev'ry honest, frank, unbiased one,
Who gives this subject any thought at all,
There is but one reply. Please mark it well:
THE TRAFFIC IN INTOXICATING DRINKS,
(THAT MEN MAY USE THEM AS A BEVERAGE)
IS ONLY EVIL, AND WITH EVIL FRAUGHT,
AND THAT CONTINUALLY.

                    This truth is seen
By weighing well some stubborn facts. And first:
DRINK MAKES OUR DRUNKARDS. Even children know
That if men **drank not** they would **not get drunk,**
And if no liquor, then no one could drink.
Oh sad the thought! and sad, because 'tis true
(For with deep shame, this truth we must confess)
That as a nation we are being turned
Most rapidly, into a set of sots.

'Tis true, we have as yet become, **not quite.**
So deeply cursed with alcoholic drinks
As have some other lands across the seas;
And yet at least a million drunkards reel
Among us, and besides, a countless host
Of mod'rate drinking Tiplers, who may well
Be styled, our "Protoplastic Debauchees."

With rapid stride, this monstrous evil stalks
Throughout our Commonwealth, and day by day
Grows stronger, boldly working out its woe.
Our population's growth, for ten years past,
Has been most rapid, yet this curse of drink
Has been increasing even faster still.
Why take the trade in beer, and that alone,
Has **more than doubled** in these ten short years.
Nor have the other drinks been far behind.

Oh! Searcher for the Truth! Lift up your eyes,
And gaze upon our cities and our towns—

Go through our streets, along our country roads,
And count those poor, deluded, wretched ones,
Who fill the ranks of that vast dismal throng
Of drunken men—alas, and women too—
Who year by year are marching down to death;—
Then tell us whence this Hell-bound army comes?
We know thy answer. O thou Voice of Truth;
"These are the children of the Demon Drink,
And by **His** traffic are these drunkards made."
No wonder then in view of all this woe,
We call this traffic wrong and **only** wrong.

III.

Again, because of its ENORMOUS WASTE
The evil of this trade is clearly seen.
The highest comprehensions of man's mind
Can never fully fathom this vast waste;
And yet by calmly looking at the facts,
We may at least learn something of the truth;
Although the whole truth, yes, the **awful truth,**
No one but God alone, can comprehend.

And first, from trusty figures it is plain,
Our Nation's drink bill for a single year
Is **seven hundred millions** in hard cash—
And latest computations make it more.
A full conception of this mighty sum
Our utmost apprehensions can not reach:
As well might we attempt to grasp God's thoughts
Or measure in our minds unending years.

Why counting ev'ry day, ten hours each,
For twenty-seven days, a man can count,
One million dollars only, yet we spend
This much, and seven hundred times as much,

Each year; for Satan's deadly damning drink.
Why this **vast sum, is** double what we pay
For taxes, in our cities, counties, States,
And in our Territories, **all** combined.

Just think of it ! We deal out **every** year,
As much hard cash for liquors, as would pay
In **less than three short years,** our public debt.
We call this waste "direct;" But let us look
A moment at that which is **"indirect."**
Five (?) hundred thousand persons are engaged,
In this vile traffic in the souls of men,
Within **the** bounds of these United States.
What do the **labors of** these men effect ?
What noble works do all these hands perform ?
Are these the builders of our people's **peace?**
The true upholders of **our nation's weal?**
The voice of Truth, in anger, thunders—" No !
These men **are really** robbers in disguise;
They murder, plunder, weaken and destroy."
Whatever else these men may say or wish,
The **out-come** of their trade is **Death and Hell.**

What would we think, if Congress should decide,
To raise an army **half a million strong,**
And send them forth to burn our crops of corn—
To slay each year, an hundred thousand souls—
To beggar happy homes, break happy hearts,
And plunge the whole land into speechless woe ?
An act like that all men would stigmatize
As **madness:** Yet this very thing we do.
Our blinded nation, for a paltry sum—
Compared with what it costs her—humbly grants
An army half a million strong, the right (?)
To waste her riches and to blast her peace.
How many millions **would** this army earn
If they should **turn** their strength to honest toil ?

Again we humbly ask of those who know (?)
How many million tons of golden grain,
And luscious fruits, are made unfit for food
By brewing and distilling deadly Drink?
Go count our whisky-paupers, if you can (?)
How many millions do we spend for them?
Go then, and search the records of our Courts,
And find from them, how much we yearly pay,
To prosecute and punish men for crimes
Which spring from this accursed trade in Drink?
Go count the days and years of shortened life.
How much, think you, we lose each year through these?
Insane Asylums visit next—and find
How many millions yearly spent in them,
For those poor idiotic creatures there
Whose brains were maddened by the Devil's Rum?
Why, at the lowest computation made,
Or that we can make—the **enormous waste**,
Direct and indirect, of this vast trade,
Must reach, each year, Two BILLIONS, or a sum
Which equals, nay exceeds, our public debt.

With almost boundless stores of treasured wealth,
How long can even WE stand all this waste?
Had not God opened wide His own full hand
And filled us with abundance—long ere this
Grim famine would have stared us in the face.

Compare our Drink-Bill with some other things:
For instance, take Ohio, and we find
She pays for Education, year by year,
About eight million dollars, more or less;
While at the same time through her " Liquor-Bill "
She worse than wastes some SIXTY MILLIONS CASH,
Almost EIGHT TIMES as much.   Oh! can it be
A State will pay for Drink eight times as much
As she expends to have her children taught?
And can the great Ohio be that State?

Again, last year, for "Foreign Mission" work,
God's people everywhere, in all the world,
Of every name and sect and nation, spent
Not quite EIGHT million dollars—while, behold!
Ohio's little State alone consumed
Some SIXTY millions in accursed Drink!
Just think! The liquor waste in one small State
Foots up almost, or quite, **eight times as much**
As all God's children give throughout the World
To send the Gospel into heathen lands.

We spend **as much** for Drink, in THREE SHORT DAYS,
In these United States—as **all the World**
Gives Christian "Foreign Missions" IN A YEAR.
Appalling thought! Well might a righteous God
Destroy us utterly for such black **sins!**

It is not strange Ohio feels this Curse,
And with a voice, three hundred thousand strong,
(Aye, more than that, had "Whiskey Leaders" dared
To fairly count the votes her people polled),
Has said in thunder **tones, "It shall be stopped."**

Ohio is not **worse, nor** yet so bad,
In fact, as many **of the** other States;
From Maine to California's vine-clad hills—
From Northern Lakes to Southern Gulf, we see
This fell Destroyer of our wealth at work.
We call **it** "WASTE," but it is worse than waste—
From every stand-point worse—for it were good,
If all these millions, which we spend for Rum,
Instead of being drank by blinded man,
Were buried in the **bosom of** the deep,
Or hurled forever **into** Hell's abyss.

IV.

Again, this trade may be arraigned as wrong,
Because it chiefly is THE CAUSE OF CRIME,
This statement is indeed self-evident;
For even those who are most void of thought,
Who read our " daily papers," clearly see,
Nay, *cannot help but see*, what prominence
Accursed liquor holds in working out
Our catalogue of criminals and crimes.
Oh Drink! Thy black, blood-curdling catalogue
Keeps up in Hell a constant jubilee,
As thy dark deeds are telegraphed below;
For demons know full well that from THEE spring
Earth's basest criminals and foulest crimes.

How often do we find some loving son,
Or tender father, or kind husband, turned
By alcohol into a frenzied fiend
Who cares not though he slays his dearest friend,
For, reeling home, with maddened brain, he bathes
His hands, it may be, in his mother's blood,
Or, seizing by the throat his faithful wife,
With fiendish grip, he strangles her to death,
Or, snatching from her breast their infant child,
He dashes out its life upon the hearth.
Let candid men go to their county-seats,
And, from the records there, count up the crimes
Which have been caused by alcoholic drinks.
We need not say what answer they will give.
The truth is, there are very few indeed
So steeped in sin, so hardened, so debased,
So lost to every principle of right,
So utterly Satanic, that they can
Commit a dreadful crime at all, unless
They have beforehand nerved themselves, to do
Their deeds of horror, by the Devil's rum.

2

Reliable statistics clearly show
That in some way, direct or indirect,
Three-fourths, if not *four-fifths* of all our crimes
Are but the bitter fruitage of the cup that kills;
The cup that sparkles, yet whose sting is death;
The cup whose beauty ends in speechless woe;
The cup whose taste leads down to endless hell;
Intoxicating Cup! Crime comes from thee!

Let those who know, tell, if they think they can,
How much the liquor traffic has to do
With all our other crimes of every grade.
For instance, with our houses of ill-fame,
Inhabited by those vile ones " whose feet
Go down to death, whose steps take hold on hell."
How much in keeping up these gambling dens
Which so infest our cities and our towns?

Oh fellow-countrymen! Intemperance
The evil of all evils surely is:
For, till God's secret things are all revealed,
No finite mind can ever fully grasp,
No finite tongue can ever truly tell,
How much of crime this most accursed trade
In drink, has laid upon our groaning globe.

V.

Our Pauperism, also, comes from drink;
At least, by far the greater part of it.
Go, visit our asylums for the poor,
And ask the inmates of these pauper homes,
Who sent you here? **Three times in every five**
The voice of truth must say: " Drink sent us here."
Whose cheerless homes are full of pinching want?
Whose half-clad children cry in vain for bread?
Whose wives weep bitter, burning tears, because

A brutal hand is often raised to strike
The trembling, frail, and unfed form of one
Whom that same hand was once so nobly pledged
To love, support, encourage, and protect?
Whose mother, with her silver hair, is brought
With sorrow to the grave, because her son
Forgets her love and sympathy and care,
And flings her from him in his drunken hate?
To all these questions there is *one* reply,
And *only* one.   It is the drunkard's home.
It is the drunkard's mother, wife, and child
Who sit and weep in penury and want,
Or groan beneath the weight of cruel blows,
Or shiv'ring, in their rags, around an empty grate,
Bemoan the bitter cold of winter's snows.
Imaginary picture this, you say?
Oh, *no*, xo, NO!   Oh, would to God it were!
But every moment just such scenes occur.
Without exaggeration we may say
That this accursed traffic in strong drink
Produces, year by year, at **least three-fourths**
Of all our pauperism.
                     But 'tis asked,
Who builds all these asylums for the poor?
Who pays these whisky " trials " in our Courts?
Who feeds these whisky paupers?   Who supports
All these, our jails and penitentiaries,
So largely filled with whisky criminals?
This is a question touching every man
Who pays his honest taxes; but we hear
Good business men and farmers sometimes say:
" Well I don't drink; my boys don't drink, therefore
This liquor business is no care of mine."
Oh, is it not?   Good sir, just stop and think.
Why are our taxes found so heavy now?
Who pays these taxes?   Do the whisky men?
Oh, no, indeed! few taxes do they pay

Compared with those their awful trade entails.
Take one fair sample, out of hundreds more;
In Cincinnati, clear statistics proved,
That during eighteen months, not long ago,*
Of crimes committed, **eighty-one per cent,**
Of them were traced *directly to strong drink;*
While at this time the city records show
That during twelve, out of these eighteen months,
Her brewers and saloonists all combined,
Paid to the city treasury a tax
Of not quite fourteen thousand dollars! Ah!
Oh, how these noble men *do help the State !* (?)
While during this same time ONE " dry goods " house,
" John Shillito and Company," alone
Paid over fourteen thousand dollars. Ah !!
Who pays the taxes flowing from saloons ?
Just think, one " dry goods " firm paid out one year
Almost a thousand dollars more for tax
Than all of Cincinnati's liquor men,
An host almost four thousand strong, all told;
Yet all this time, upon the Sabbath day,
This same great " dry goods " house must close its doors
While all those " grog shops " were allowed to ply,
With double zeal, their trade of woe and death,
Upon God's holy, sacred day of rest.

Has Justice fled for ever from the earth ?
Is Satan king of all that he surveys ?
Arise! Oh gracious God, and plead Thy cause,
And open Thou the eyes of blinded men!
Then shall we see how we are cursed by rum,
And rising in Thy might we'll cast it off,
Nor longer suffer honest men to bear
The heavy burdens of the Liquor League.
Yet such is now the case, for everywhere

* 1880-1.

The heavy end of all our taxes rests—
Not on the liquor men, by any means,
From whose vile work these taxes chiefly spring—
But on the honest tillers of the soil,
And those who by hard work procure their bread.
How long shall we submit to this base fraud,
And groan beneath these taxes caused by drink?
Good sir, you surely will no longer say:
" This liquor business is no care of mine."

But surely there are some *great benefits*
Resulting from this traffic, to off-set
All these enormous evils,—are there not?
Or else a nation claiming common-sense
Would never tolerate it for a day.
We ask, where are these wondrous benefits?
At least two billion dollars of our gold
Drained from our country every year ask, " Where?"
Our million drunkards' thickened tongues ask, "Where?"
Two million wives and mothers, pale and sad,
With weeping eyes and bleeding hearts, ask, "Where?"
Three million helpless children, clad in rags,
With hungry lips, ask drunken parents, " Where?"
By hundred thousands, paupers ask us " Where?"
Ten thousands, groaning in a felon's cell,
Or waiting for the hangman's rope, ask, "Where?"
By thousands, insane drunkards shriek out, "Where?"
That drunkard host, one hundred thousand strong,
Which marches slowly, surely, year by year,
Into the yawning mouth of Hell, asks, "Where?"
By day and night, those wailing, writhing hosts
Of liquor dealers and of drunkards " cast
Into the Lake of Fire," from out the flames,
With blistered tongues, are asking, "Where, oh, WHERE
Are all those *boasted benefits* of rum?"
An echo, rolling back from Heaven, Earth,
And Hell, forever answers, " WHERE, OH, WHERE?"

PART II.

PROPOSED REMEDIES.

"Shall the throne of iniquity have fellowship with thee, which
frameth mischief by a law?"—Psa. xciv. 20.

I.

We come to notice next, some of the plans,
Which nations have adopted, to restrain
The evils of this most accursed trade,
At **least** within, some so-called proper bounds.
All nations stamp, this trade in drink **as** wrong.
No nation, worthy **of the** name; to-day,
Allows free trade in liquors. Everywhere
The traffic is *restricted* (?) *in some way.*
Now that restriction, most of all employed,
We call **a** "LICENSE" LAW And all such laws,
Are based, upon a common principle.

It would not do for all, to sell strong drink
Without restriction; Therefore, says the state,
To any—who will pay a given sum,
" We grant to you, the privilege (?) to sell
Intoxicating drinks: And *only* those
This priv'lege have, who pay the sum prescribed.
—Oh! sweet, sweet, privilege! to murder men;
To ruin homes, and manufacture woe.

Despite, **the** countless lies, of liquor men,
This **proposition,** can be clearly proved:

THAT LICENSE LAWS HAVE FAILED—MUST ALWAYS FAIL
TO SWEEP AWAY THE EVILS OF STRONG DRINK.

No one need tell us, that these laws *have* failed;
For facts, we cannot gainsay or deny,
Compel us to admit, that they have failed.
The drink trade never was so great as now,
On every hand it flourishes and spreads,
Beneath the gentle sway, of license laws.
For centuries, these laws, have *seemed* to try,
To stop Intemperance.   What have they done?
Have they once checked this ever growing tide,
Or raised a ripple, on its topmost wave?
Truth answers: No!   **But Alcohol is king.**
And sways a wider scepter; day by day;
While at his throne, new drunkards daily bow,
And blindly kiss the rod, by which they die.

Our "Revenue" statistics, clearly show:
How wondrous, is this giant traffic's growth.
Take beer alone.   And these statistics say:
Just fifteen years ago;* we only made
Two hundred million gallons, of this stuff:
These same statistics say, we made almost,
Six hundred million gallons, this past year.†
Thus has our trade in beer, been multiplied
Almost three-fold, in only fifteen years.
Oh, License Laws!   How wondrous your success!
Behold what you have done, in fifteen years!
Would any marvel, if some simple soul
Should ask, "How long I wonder will it take,
To swamp the liquor traffic, at this rate?"

Nor is it true, as some make bold to say,
That "beer and other lighter liquors, tend
To drive out stronger liquors,"   For we know,
That all these so-called, "lighter drinks," create

* 1870–71.   † 1885–86.

A taste for stronger liquors, and in fact,
Distilled, and all our strongest drinks—like beer—
Are year by year, increasing more and more,
Although, not quite, at such a rapid rate.
In view of all these facts, Oh, License Laws!
We would in all humility, inquire,
How many generations it will be,
Before you free us from king Alcohol?
To judge from *present* progress; Do you think,
That it will be before the Judgment day?

II.

But some may ask—as many often do—
Will not wise (?) stringent License laws suppress,
The wrongs of strong drink? Must they always fail?
We most unhesitatingly reply:
That as they always have failed in the past,
So in the future, they must always fail.
And First: They fail, because such laws ARE WRONG.
We have already seen, that this great trade
In liquors; as a beverage, is wrong;
And *only* wrong, and *always must* be wrong;
We now take one more step, and boldly say:
No NATION HAS A RIGHT TO LICENSE WRONG.
When any state, grants license to a crime;
By virtue of that fact, it thence becomes,
A partner in that crime, and must of course,
Protect it, by its officers and laws;
Now this vile traffic, being wrong, IS CRIME
Against the race; against a Holy God;
And should be treated, just like other crimes.
A state might just as well—and better too—
Grant " licenses " to prostitution, theft,
To murder or to treason, as to Drink;
For license it; *then " licensed " are all these.*
And every other, nameless, shameless crime.

What would we think, if some state should enact,
Some laws to " regulate" the crime of theft,
Like those to regulate the Liquor Crime ?
Suppose our Government should say to thieves.
(All those who have " *good moral characters* ")
Good Sirs! If you will pay in to the state
Each year, *as revenue*, a given sum;
The Government, will license you to steal,
And plunder, all your friends and neighbors; **but,**
You can't steal everything;   It would not do.
You must be " regulated" by just (?) laws,
These wise restraints you must observe: to wit,
You shall not steal upon the Sabbath day;
Nor shall you steal, in any case, from those
Who have not reached, the age of twenty-one;
And most of all, be sure, you never steal,
From those, who have become " *habitual* thieves."
How would we look upon such laws?   And yet,
Such laws as these, if passed in every state,
Would not produce, one-half the bitter woo
And poverty and ignorance and sin,
As do these most accursed, " License laws,"
Nor in the sight of God, would they be worse.
The truth is: Liquor license laws are wrong,
All wrong; nor can they ever be made right?
No wonder such laws fail.   They *ought* to fail.

Again we claim, these License laws must fail;
Because THEY ARE UNJUST.   They help the few;
But curse the many.   We should like to know:
By what right any Commonwealth, can say,
To certain classes, of her citizens—
And from the very nature of the case,
Her lowest, meanest, vilest classes too—
Give me a share, of these ill-gotten gains;
And you shall have the privilege (?) to sell
Intoxicating drinks, and none else shall ?"

2*

Suppose a stringent license law is passed,
And (were it not IMPOSSIBLE) enforced
So strictly, that it would completely drive,
The last unlicensed dealer from the trade;
How long then would it be, till we should hear:
On every side the cry, " Monopoly,"
" Class Legislation." What else would it be?
If—as a bev'rage—it is right, to sell
These vile intoxicating drinks, to men;
Then ALL should have the right, to ply the trade,
But if 'tis *wrong*, then NONE should have such right.

But from " financial" stand-points, view this trade,
And see: If " Justice" sits enthroned on high,
While " Madam" License wears the royal crown?
We ask who profits, by this giant trade?
It surely cannot be the drunken sot,
Whose reeling form, is clad in filthy rags?
It surely cannot be, his wretched wife,
Nor yet his children, poor and pale and starved?
It surely cannot be the Government;
For everyone, who thinks a moment, knows;
That every year, our nation pays far more,
For liquor paupers, criminals and crimes,
Than she receives, from liquor revenues,
Large as these wicked revenues may be.
We ask, once more, who profits, by this trade?
'Tis not the drunkard; nor his wife nor child;
'Tis not the Government. Who is it then?
Truth sends us back this answer: It must be;
The Liquor Dealer. (**May God pity him.**)
Intrenched behind the legal ramparts, raised
Around him, by our blinded Government;
He reaps, the awful riches, of his trade.
But Oh! at what a fearful price; For Christ
The Savior asks: " What shall it profit men,
To gain the whole world, yet to lose their souls?"

But let us, for the sake of argument,
Agree to call, all these ill-gotten gains,
A benefit, to these duped liquor men.
Admitting this; we ask: But is it JUST,
That only ONE man should get all the gains
In any trade, while FIFTY men, must pay
His bills, and pocket nothing in return?
Now there are not, one million liquor men
As dealers, in this country; and we ask
In candor: Is it *fair?* or is it *just?*
To see, one million people in our land,
Arrayed in gorgeous splendor, rolled in wealth,
Their wishes, all supplied, at the expense
Of fifty millions, of their fellow-men?
And when, especially, for all this wealth,
They dole out nothing in return, but woe,
And sorrow, anguish, poverty and pain,
Disease and shame and crime, despair and death,
Both in this world, and in the world to come?
Can this be "justice?" Whisky men are loud,
To shriek, for their pretended "liberties,"
And shout, for "Justice," and for "Equal Rights."

Awake! Ye honest tillers, of the soil!
Assert YOUR rights! Which in the past have been
Vast wrongs. Thank God! The time is coming fast,
When all these noble sons of toil, who brave
A burning sun, or face a fiery forge,
Shall cease to feed and foster, bloated beer
And brandy Bar-room Keepers. But they, too,
Will lift up earnest voices, and **demand,**
Some "Equal Rights" and "Justice" for themselves.
Our Liquor "License Laws" are *most unjust.*
No wonder, God writes "FAILURE" on them all.

III.

Again; these laws to License Liquor fail,
Because, THEY WERE **NOT MADE TO** BE ENFORCED.
We might suspect this from **the** well-known fact:
That Liquor Dealers, almost to a man,
Desire and urge, "judicious (?) License Laws."
Nor **is** it strange they should; for "License" makes
The Government a PARTNER in **their** trade,
And thereby renders it, with all its crime
And **woe**, not only **lawful,** but alas!
Respectable; at least to some degree.
There **are, no** doubt, great numbers of **good men,**
Who earnestly and honestly believe,
That stringent license laws can be enforced,
And will remove the evils of strong drink.
But surely, all, by this time ought **to see,**
That license laws *are made by liquor men*,
And always get their chief support, from those
Who hope **to** profit by the traffic's growth.
We boldly say, that for the last ten years,
In **these** United **States, the greater** part
Of "Temp'rance" (?) Legislative **acts, by far,**
Were not intended, **to** suppress **the** wrongs,
Of this great Liquor Traffic; but were passed,
By liquor men; to legalize their trade:
Or else; to lull to sleep, the consciences,
And thus secure the **votes of** Temp'rance **men.**
If this be true, AND IT IS TRUE. How can
A License Law, remove the liquor trade?
It can't. It is IMPOSSIBLE it should.
We might as well attempt, **to drill a hole**
With *turnips*, through the Andes **or the Alps;**
As try to sweep away, this **liquor** trade,
By "Licensing" and bidding it God speed,)
In all its blighting, with'ring, deadly work.

No! No!! These license laws, will never cure
Intemperance; for they are wholly *wrong;*
They are *unjust;* and *cannot be enforced.*
Hence in the Future; just as in the Past,
These silly laws, will evermore be found,
To be manipulated, **by their friends.**
And Fellow-Countrymen! When we shall see;
The Liquor Dealer, rising in his might,
To put this liquor traffic down, we may,
(With wond'ring eyes and bated breath) be sure;
That we are basking, in the dawning light,
Which shall announce, the Earth's "Millenial Morn."

But in respect, to all the bitter wrongs
Of this whole "License System;" let us give,
The reins of judgment, into Reason's hands;
And temper wrath, with justice and with truth,
Then, *well* does it behoove, the greater part,
Of those who advocate the Temp'rance Cause,
To cast the mantle of their charity,
Around the man who sells the deadly stuff,
As well as 'round the one, who takes his dram,
Of course *both* men are wrong, most deeply wrong;
But let us ask ourselves: Have we clean skirts?
Are we completely innocent? Have we
Not voted "license" now for many years,
And thus been tacit partners, in these wrongs?

The drunkard constantly, commits a *crime.*
The drunkard-maker, still a **greater crime;**
But we believe the Government commits,
The GREATEST CRIME OF ALL, in licensing
And legalizing, this our greatest curse.
But who have made our Government? We ask,
'Tis answered: "Under God, the people have."
Then, WE—THE PEOPLE. are the most to blame.

" We: WE—The People, have been most remiss
In duty." Yes! We **pray** for Temp'rance: But—
WE VOTE—WE VOTE for WHISKY, RUM AND BEER.
In mercy, may our God forgive this wrong;
And grant us grace, henceforth, to set it right.

IV.

Still more: Not only License Laws have failed;
But every other **half-way** measure fails.
For it is certain **that** there never can,
Be any COMPROMISE, between the **Truth**
And Error; God and Satan; Heav'n and Hell.
Hence, "Civil-Damage" **Laws**, "Taxation" **Laws**,
Or even "Local-Option" Laws, must fail,
To cure the evils of Intemperance.

Take "Civil-Damage" Laws, such as they **have,**
In quite a number of our leading States,
Which make the Liquor-seller liable,
To answer, for the wrongs and lawless deeds,
Of those made drunken, by his dreadful drink.
The inconsistencies, of such a law,
Will always, clearly, make it null and void.
As if the Liquor-seller could atone,
(Provided, always, you can prove his guilt,
And legally convict him) **with** his gold.
For ruined homes and **lives**; for broken hearts;
For maidens ravished, through the drunkard's lusts;
For honest men shot down, by drunken sots;
For daughters driven to a life of shame;
For sons made felons, through the love of drink;
For friends and children, sisters, mothers, **wives,**
Whose swollen eyes, bespeak their blighted hopes,
Whose bitter tears, burn furrows down their cheeks,
While blank despair, eats out their aching hearts.

Oh! Drunkard-Maker! Can you PAY for these?
Can all your blood-bought wealth, wipe out these tears?
Or pour the balm of joy into these hearts?
Or build again, these desolated homes?
Or bring dead drunkards' souls up out of hell?
How silly for a State to "license" men
To do some fearful wrong; and then turn round,
And punish them because they do that wrong!
What father sends his boys to work, and then
Turns in and flogs them when their work is done?
No wonder "Civil-Damage" laws have failed.

Again, on every side, we hear the cry:
"TAXATION; let us try taxation laws."
Well, let us see, just what taxation means,
Applied to this infernal liquor trade.
And First. It means PROTECTION to the trade.
When any State imposes any tax,
Upon a trade, she thereby guarantees
Protection to that trade, within her bounds.
She makes herself a sharer, in its gains,
And grants to it, the sanction of her law.
Now if that trade is wrong, she shares that wrong,
And *must* protect it, if it pays its tax.

Again, taxation laws, are all unjust,
Because such laws, are really license laws;
But with another name. Now this is clear,
When we reflect: That though it *seems* most fair;
And *seems* to open this great trade to all;
And *seems* to say, " Come one; come all alike,
And pay your tax, and sell your gin and beer;"
Yet is it fair? What are the stubborn facts?
Who buy these tax receipts, to sell strong drink?
Who really do engage in this vile trade? ·
Wherever such taxation laws exist?
Do noble men, the bravest, and the best?

Do honest men, who seek their neighbors' good?
Do Christian men, who fear to grieve their God,
Who long, to point the sinner to the Cross,
And tell the story of their Savior's love?
Do these, take out a Liquor Dealer's tax?
As soon take out a tax to sell Hell Fire;
Or traffic in a brother's blood; as sell
Intoxicating drinks, to ruin men.
We see at once: All noble, great and good,
All worthy men, all truly honest men;
All those grand Christian men, who fear their God,
Who are the very best men in our land;
Would never think of taking out a tax,
To buy and sell, intoxicating drinks.
Hence, all such men, are shut out from the trade,
And from the very nature of the case,
Must always be shut out! Who then in fact
Have charge, of this great drunkard-making trade,
According to this plan, of taxing it?
We answer: as a rule, the worst of men;
For good men will not stain their hands with rum.
But wicked men; (Alas! and women, too,)
Quite often, thieves and prostitutes and knaves
Who break alike, the laws of God and man;
Who desecrate the Sabbath's sacred rest,
And seek with ribald song, and drunken jest,
To make themselves believe, there is no God.
These are the men and women, who can say:
We fear not God, nor yet regard we man;
So we will pay this tax, and take this trade,
And God can Heaven have, and Satan hell;
But as for us, we'll have our gin and beer.".
Ye blinded States! Who tax this Godless trade!
Oh! Will you never see, that by such tax
You pay a **premium** to vice and crime?
You really say, to those who are so base,
That they are willing, for its tear-stained wealth,

To sell strong drink. " Here is this mighty trade,
With all its wondrous profits; Pay your tax;
And you can sell your whisky and your beer."
Now *only* those who pay their tax *can* sell;
And *good* men *will* not; Thus the state *creates*,
A vast monopoly, for wicked men.

But some say: We will make the tax so high,
We'll tax the trade to death. You might as well
Attempt to tax the Wicked One to death.
No! Never can this Drunkard Curse be cured,
By so-called " Taxing Laws." For every state
Which taxes, this "Gigantic crime of crimes;"
In fact, grants "license" to our greatest curse,
And shares the profits of its Godless gains.
Let those who advocate taxation laws,
Remember, that an holy God will hold,
Each State, which taxes this great wickedness,
Accountable, for every dollar drained,
From this vile trade, which reeks with human gore.

V.

Still further; many advocate those laws
Called, "SUNDAY-CLOSING" acts, to stop this trade
On Sabbath-days, like other trades are stopped.
Well, *in the end*, such laws must always fail,
In their enforcement, and in their effect.
At best they only compromise with sin.
Stop dram-shops, only on the Sabbath-day,
And you must "license" them through all the week.
You stop them *one* day—legalize them *six;*
Whereas, they *should* be stopped all seven days.
Now in a government, as free as ours,
How do these "Sunday liquor laws" succeed?
Just go and ask Ohio or New York.

Will men who violate the law all week,
Not break it on the Sabbath if they can?
These Liquor-Dealers are a lawless set,
They ALL transgress the laws of God; and more
They, as a rule, defy the laws of man.
There's not a liquor-shop, in all the land,
When it is plying its infernal trade,
That does not, daily, violate the law,
In spirit, or in letter, or in both.
These liquor men will argue: "If 'tis right
To sell all week; it can't be very wrong
To sell some on a Sunday." First, we find
Their back doors open; soon, they grow more bold,
And fling their front doors open, and defy,
The laws, they long have trampled under foot.
What care such men for "Sunday-Closing" laws?
For six days, legalize their wicked trade,
And you may rest assured, no "Sunday-law"
Will stop these servants of the Demon Drink,
Or even check them in their mad career.
A Sabbath law is right; and would to God!
We had such Sabbath laws, as would compel,
All men to pay, at least some due respect,
To this sweet, sacred, precious day of rest;
The day God loves; The day tired nature needs;
The day, for which our fathers risked their lives,
That they might bring it to these Western wilds,
And make it here, our nation's corner-stone;
The bulwark, of our nation's liberties;
The anchor of our nation's destiny.
By all means, let us have our Sabbath laws,
And make God's day, indeed a day of rest.
But let us bear in mind, that "Sunday laws,"
Which license liquor selling all the week,
Will never stop it on the Sabbath day.
Let Sabbath laws, be Sabbath laws indeed;
But let us never pass a whisky law,

And cloak it with the Sabbath's sacred name.
All dram-shop " Sunday-closing " laws are wrong,
Which sanction liquor selling through the week.

Again great numbers of good Temp'rance men,
Think " LOCAL OPTION " is the very thing,
To free us from the thraldom of strong drink.
Although 'tis true, such laws have many friends,
Yet even " Local Option " laws must fail.
They are a compromise with sin;   Because
Their main foundation principle is wrong:
For in effect, they say; that it is right,
To do the wrong, if those who wish the wrong,
Can only get a clear majority;
In other words;   In case the people vote,
In any given city, ward or town,
To license this accursed liquor trade,
The state, must then, accede to their demand.
Whereas to " license " drink at any time,
In any place, is wrong, and always wrong.
Hence every argument, which lies against,
A " license " law, will likewise lie against,
A " Local Option " law.   We have such laws,
In sev'ral states; but have they banished Rum ?
They have succeeded, somewhat in the South,
And in some favored places in the North;
But taken on the whole, these laws have failed.
Take Massachusetts; and what do we find ?
The " Whiskyites " can't carry every town,
They therefore go to those they can control,
And getting " license " there, they then supply
The thirsty souls, in neighb'ring " Temp'rance towns,"
And laughing in their sleeves, the cup goes round.
And what is worse, these " Local Option " laws,
Fail chiefly, where we need them, most of all.
That is: In cities, and our larger towns.
If even in a little " County Seat,"

One ward votes whisky;   You can never make,
That County seat, a strictly Temp'rance town.
How futile then, must "Local Option" be,
In Brooklyn, Boston, Pittsburgh or New York,
Chicago, Philadelphia, Washington,
In Cincinnati or in Baltimore,
In San Francisco or in New Orleans.

VI.

"High License" is the constant cry of some:
  As though God might be bought with larger bribes!
Would we, "High License" murder, treason, theft?
Would we, "High License" bribery or lust?
We shrink with horror from so vile a thought.
Yet many would, forsooth, "High License" Rum,
Which largely causes all these horrid crimes.

Suppose our Nation's Statesmen should decide,
" Polygamy in Utah can't be stopped,
  But from it we can get vast revenues
  Which poured into our treasury, will help
Pay taxes, and reduce our public debt.
We'll not prohibit this most loathsome curse,
But we'll " High License " it, and this will drive
All those who cannot pay our heavy tax,
Out of the business.   This of course won't stop,
But surely will restrict (?) Polygamy.
We'll pass for Utah this " High License " law,
You Mormons, if you marry twice you shall,
Pay down, one thousand dollars, in gold coin
Into the coffers of our government;
If three times, then five thousand is the sum;
If four times, then ten thousand must be paid;
And if you pay a " License " extra high,
One hundred thousand dollars, you may wed

Whole " Female Seminaries " at a time."
How would we all regard a law like that ?

High License reaches only one result.
It does not check Drink's traffic in the least,
It simply puts it into fewer hands;
Men who are keener brained, and longer pursed
And therefore villians of a deeper dye.
But this one thing is sure. It does intrench
This whole vile traffic in accursed Drink,
Behind Tax Payers' sordid selfishness.
For though it does not lessen her saloons,
It does pay to the State large revenues;
Hence many sober but short-sighted men
Imagine selfishly, that these will pay
Their taxes. But they should remember this:
That while " High License " revenues are large
The vast expenses of Drink's traffic are
Far larger. Is this true economy
For every dollar saved to pay out ten ?
Besides, " High License " gives to liquor lords
This plea; which they assert, entitles them
To gratitude, protection and respect.
We are," say they, " the pillars of the State,
We pave your streets, and beautify your parks,
We build" (and fill) " your jails and City Halls,
And pay the teachers in your public schools;
Why, were it not for our useful trade,
The State's expenses, never could be paid."
And many silly men will say, " That's so.
There's no sense in this cry, ' SALOONS MUST GO.' "
Such was the Liquor Dealers' constant claim,
Before Atlanta fought her gallant fight,
But now we find she never prospered so,
Nor have her taxes ever been so low.

The Devil never dares to give a dose
Of error, pure and simple, for he knows

We would reject it. Hence he always tries
To find some truth, with which to sugar-coat
His deadly pills of error. Then he comes
Just as he did to mother Eve—and cries,
Here, this is just the very thing you need.
We look. We taste. It looks and tastes all right.
We swallow—when alas! we find, too late,
We've taken unawares, the Devil's drugs.
Now if he ever laid a hellish snare,
With which to utterly delude our race,
We find it in this dread " High License fraud,"
Which he has sugar-coated with this truth;
" A half a loaf is better than no bread."
The awful error hidden here: is this.
YOUR HALF LOAF'S POISONED. Poisoned with the blood
Of millions slain by Hell's infernal Rum;
'Tis stained with tears so bitter, that most sweet
Compared with them, would be, Earth's wormwood and
    its gall.
Would such half loaf, or slice, or single crumb
Be better for us than no bread at all?
No! No! High License, is the Devil's snare,
And of it let all Temp'rance men beware.
An ounce of fact, is worth far more, than tons
Of untried theories. What are the facts?
Go to Nebraska, and some other States.
Go to Chicago. Other cities too;
Where they have tested these "High License" laws,
And you will find: They have completely failed,
To stop the rampant ravages of Rum.

When some drunk husband, beats his helpless wife,
And turns her, and their children, out of doors,
To weep and shiver in the sleet or snow,
Of some cold, stormy, bitter, wintry night;
Oh! Will it comfort those poor weeping ones?
Oh! Will it clothe those, half-clad shiv'ring forms?

Oh! will it heal and soothe, those brutal stripes,
Upon the back of that true loving wife?
Oh! will it bring back gladness to their hearts,
At such a time, to know, that he who sold
The dreadful drink, which made their father drunk,
And made that husband, once so kind, a brute,
Has paid, into the county treasury,
A THOUSAND DOLLARS FOR HIS "LICENSE?" *Shame!*
Oh! **Shame!!** on any government or State,
Which can be ruled or bribed, by hellish Rum
At any price, to desolate its homes;
Oppress its helpless and defenceless ones;
To live in luxury, upon the wealth,
Drawn from its people's wretchedness and woe!!!

But will "High License" stop this curse of drink?
No! Never!! Possibly it may shut up,
A FEW gin-mills, which cannot pay the tax.
But it will scarcely lessen, in the least,
The quantities of liquor, sold and drank.
These liquors may be sold by fewer men;
(And from that very fact, all men can see,
The State creates a vile Monopoly.)
But will they be less deadly in their work?
Will all their sorrow be less hard to bear?
Will bitter tears be sweeter to the taste,
Because they were wrung out, at greater cost?

Ye Temp'rance Workers! Do not be deceived.
Oh! **Never, Never**, advocate again!
This most high-handed compromise with Hell.
Let so-called and pretended Temp'rance men
Be champions of this measure, if they wish.
But let us not be caught, with Satan's hook,
By gulping down this most deceitful bait.

Nor will the "MORAL-SUASION" cure avail,
To stay this Plague, as many seem to think.

Why, we have tried this Moral-Suasion salve,
For more than fifty years, and yet this Plague
Of Drunkenness, is spreading all the time.

Why did the "Washingtonian Movement" fail?
Why did the "Murphy" methods, not succeed?
Nay, more: Why did that "God-Inspired Crusade"
Of holy women, fail to sweep away,
The firm foundations, from beneath strong drink?
It was because they rested all their hope,
On Moral Suasion, and on that *alone.*
Now all admit, that these grand "movements" did
Accomplish much; and were the stepping-stones
To better things. Yet after all they failed
To kill this Demon, with their "Moral-Suasion" guns.

Now Moral Suasion's good; nor can we have,
Too much of it. But it is not enough.
We need some kind of "legal suasion," too;
And this is gotten only at the "polls."
We Temp'rance men must *vote* as well as pray.
How can God hear us, though on bended knees,
We lift our hands on high, and plead with Him,
To stay this Plague; when at that very time,
These same uplifted hands are stained with blood,
Through open partnership with this great Curse,
By "license" granted at the ballot-box?
Do *actions* not speak louder than mere words?
What cares the Liquor-Dealer for our prayers,
Our "Moral Suasion," or our bitter tears,
Our broken hearts, our desolated homes,
While he can flaunt his "License" in our face,
And claim the strong protection of the law?
No! No!! Mere Moral Suasion (it is true
May save some drunkards, but) can never turn,
The Drunkard-Maker from his wicked work,
While God's own children "legalize" his trade.

Oh! Thou, most gracious God; Omnipotent;
All-wise, Eternal, changeless, just and good,
Most Loving, Holy, Pitiful and True!
Thine Endless Being, far beyond all bounds,
Transcends all space above the highest Heav'n,
And sinking down, beneath the lowest Hell,
Goes down and down, till all is lost but Thee.
Thou guidest ALL. Each atom and each sun.
All Angels, Devils, good and wicked men.

Oh! Thou, Great God! We lift our hearts to thee;
And in the name of Christ, our Lord, Thy Son,
We plead, that in Thine own good time and way,
Thou wouldst remove this Curse of Drunkenness.
Oh! God! Enlighten us, and let Thy Truth
Enlarge our hearts; we put our hands in Thine;
Oh! Father! Lead us, guide us in Thy way!
And teach Thy children, Lord, to see how vain
It is, to try to compromise with sin!
And grant, that soon we all may realize,
That EVERY HALF-WAY MEASURE, to destroy
This traffic, in the "worm that never dies"
Will only end in ruin and defeat,
And bring down on our heads, Thy righteous wrath.

Then lead us to THY REMEDY, Oh! Lord!
Oh! Fill us with the Holy Spirit's grace!
Oh! Gird us for our COMING CONFLICT's strife!
Be Thou our Captain, in this holy war,
And soon, King Alcohol shall "lick the dust,"
And Thou shalt have the praise forevermore,
Through Him, who loved us, and who gave Himself
To die for us, we ask it all—AMEN.

PART III.

THE TRUE REMEDY.

"Thanks be to God, Who giveth us the victory through our Lord, Jesus Christ."—I Cor. xv: 57.

I.

And now, this greatest question of the age,
So practical; so fraught with weal or woe,
To every nation, and to all the race;
Is pressed straight home, upon **our** minds and hearts.
We cannot shirk **the** issue, if **we** would,
Nor can we shut our eyes to this plain fact;
That all our **half-way** measures, are a snare;
For all **our** COMPROMISING SCHEMES HAVE FAILED,
And Drink's deep curse, is daily growing **worse.**
What shall we do? **Is** there no remedy
For this gigantic wrong? "Is there no balm
In Gilead? Is no physician **there?"**
Yes, blessed be our God! **there** is a cure,
For this great Curse of Curses, Crime of Crimes.
There is **one** remedy, and **only one.**
There is but one effective cure for crime,
And that is PROHIBITION. And we hold
That nothing short of utter and complete
" *Tee-to-tal* " *prohibition*, of this trade
In liquors (as **a** beverage) **can free**
Us from the thralldom, of the Demon Drink.
This prohibition, must be framed BY LAW;

And in the Constitution of our States,
And of the whole United States be placed:
And in God's own good time, it shall be done.

To "Prohibition" many men object:
Of these men, some are good.   But note this fact;
That every member of the "Liquor League"
Is eager to denounce "this foolish scheme
Of Prohibition" as another name
For madness; and on every side, we hear
Them urge, all sorts of silly sophistries,
To prove it both fanatical and vain.
Now notice some of those objections made
To Prohibition; and please WEIGH THEM WELL.

And First, they say: "That this whole question is,
A MORAL QUESTION, and we cannot take;
These moral questions into "Politics."
There never was a more profound mistake.
This is a moral question, it is true;
And so was Slavery.   Did we succeed
In keeping Slav'ry out of "Politics?"
No more can this great question be kept out.
In "politics" we find the very place
For Temperance.   And when men learn to vote,
As well as pray, for Prohibition; then,
And not 'till then, will Rum's full doom be sealed.

Much more consistent are the "liquor" men.
Do they keep "whisky" out of politics?
If so.   Why have our "two Great (?) Parties" kept,
For years; almost as silent as the grave,
Concerning this great question?   Why is it
That nearly all our leading "Journals" cry,
"Away with Prohibition," while so oft
They laud the Liquor Dealers to the skies?
Why do our "Politicians" dread to touch

This question, even with a finger's tip?
'Tis easy told. THEY FEAR THE LIQUOR VOTE.
They know full well, that all these " whisky " men
Vote *solidly*, against all Temp'rance laws;
Whereas, if they can keep this question still;
The " sheepish " Temp'rance men, will follow on,
And sticking to their " whisky Parties," strive
To put a stop to this great traffic's curse,
By Moral Suasion, and by prayers and tears.

Oh!   Friends of Temp'rance (God's own holy Cause),
Let us learn wisdom, from these liquor men,
And follow them, at least, in *one* respect:
And let us cease henceforth to give support,
To any Party, which opposes us.
We Temp'rance men (one might well think) are like
The old ox, " Dobbins," roaming in the field.
To see him in his freedom, some might say
" That great strong ox, will never bend his neck,
To wear a galling yoke. Oh no! Not he!
Why what's more free, than he ? "   But bring his yoke,
And hold it up, and crack your whip, and shout:
" Come under, Dobbins," and the good old ox,
Will meekly thrust his neck, beneath the yoke.
Just so; we Temp'rance men, pray earnestly,
" Between Elections " for the Temp'rance cause:
But when " The Grand Old Parties " draw the lines,
And as is usual, at " Election times ",
Begin to " crack the Party whip," and shout
" Come under, Dobbins."   Then we Temp'rance men,
Most meekly bow our necks beneath the yoke,
March to the " polls " and vote the very same
Old " Whisky ticket."   While the Liquor men
With blandest smiles, say: " Yes, that's right; THAT's
    RIGHT;
Keep ' Moral Measures ' out of Politics."
The plainest dictates, of our common sense,

All lead us to suppose, that if good men,
Left Politics (the " science of true government ")
Entirely in the hands, of wicked men,
They would pervert it, to their own base ends.

Away! with this false doctrine, that good men,
And Moral Measures, have no proper place
In Party Politics.   Sad! Sad! the day!
When of our Land; it may be truly said:
" The Just and Good, are trampled under foot,
And Wicked men have full control."
For always, " Righteousness lifts nations up,
But sin, will bring reproach, to any Land."

II.

Well now, what else do Liquor-Dealers say ?
Their pretexts, call to mind the story told,
About a certain farmer, who had gone
Out to his barn, and chancing to look up,
He saw his " hired hand " had hung himself
Fast to the rafters in the barn; he stopped;
He gazed with horror, caught his breath; then cried,
" Well what on this earth will that man do next?"
So list'ning to these whisky arguments,
One sometimes, sits and wonders, well what next ?
Well next, beside themselves with rage, they shout;
" MEN ALWAYS HAVE DBANK, AND THEY ALWAYS WILL."

In answer to this claim so often made;
At least this much, with reason, may be said.
It does not follow, that because a wrong,
Has wrought its woe in all the ages past;
That it must still continue, through all time.
Our God is slow to wrath; He suffers long;
And patiently, holds back His thunder-bolts;

Till all His people's prayers and cries **are heard**;
Till all their "tears are bottled"; Till **the** cup,
The bitter cup, of that great wrong is full:
And then it is, He rises in His might,
And making bare, His own almighty arm;
With one fell stroke, this long permitted wrong
Is smitten; never more to curse the **World**.

How was it, in the case of Slavery?
For **it,** this same great cry was often raised;
" Slaves have been, therefore, slaves must always be."
But that great God who sits in Heaven, spoke.
" The chains of slavery shall clank no **more**:
This cup is full; My time has come." **He rose**;
He broke those shackles, and the world **is FREE**.
Just so; with this **accursed** liquor woe:
Its doom is sealed: Its cup is almost full:
A few more precious lives, and **prayers** and tears,
A **few** more battles, and perhaps **defeats**;
THEN COMES THE VICTORY; for God will rise,
And soon His red hot thunder-bolts, will fall:
Alas for those on whom they fall! For who
Can save, when once **His** wrath begins to burn,
Which has so long been slumb'ring **in** His breast?

Oh! blinded, foolish liquor men! Beware!
There **is** a just and holy God on High:
Although for ages, you have cursed the world,
Yet now your time is short. We counsel you
To quit this wicked traffic, **ere** the stroke
Of God's hot hand shall hurl you into Hell.
Oh! would; that all these blinded eyes might see!
And these hard hearts, might make their peace with God;
Might **taste His love,** before they feel His wrath;
Might **fly to Him, before it is** too late.

III.

Again, we hear these "whiskyites" exclaim:
But " PROHIBITION CANNOT BE ENFORCED,
IT IS A FAILURE, where it has been tried·"
This is the thread-bare cry on every hand;
In Corner Groceries, and in saloons,
In drug stores, grog shops, and low dogeries,
In liquor houses, wholesale and retail,
In breweries, and in distilleries;
In fact, wherever Alcohol is King;
This cry is raised, by every whisky "pimp"
And every "tippler," all beer-guzzling bloats,
All drunkards reeling to their wretched homes,
All those vile hypocrites, who loudly claim
To be the very best of Temp'rance men,
And yet who like their " toddy," and slip 'round
Quite frequently, through some saloon's back door,
And take a " dram or two," and often more,
In order to be friendly with "the boys."
All whisky " papers " subsidized by rum,
(Their name is legion) who bow blindly down,
And for the Liquor Dealers' gold, consent
To lick the very dust beneath their feet,
And at their bidding, publish all their lies:
All weak-kneed politicians, who have felt,
The power of the mighty " liquor Ring,"
Who have no manhood, to oppose the wrong,
Or battle for the right; all these alike,
Bow down and worship, at Rum's shrine of sin;
They line their pockets, with its blood-stained gold,
And with unblushing shame, its lies repeat;
These are the classes, that with tearful eyes
Are crying: " Prohibition can't succeed
But it is an 'utter failure' everywhere."
We ask, How could it possibly be worse,

With " Prohibition laws " than it is now,
Beneath the wise (?) restraints of " License laws? "
Why anyone, of any age or sex,
At any time or place, can get strong drink,
If they have money? as things now exist;
(Unless it is behind our prison walls (?).)
Then how could Prohibition make it worse,
If it should really " altogether fail ? "

But only give us Prohibition once,
And we would make at least, this grand exchange.
Upon our " Statute books " would be inscribed,
A just and holy law, instead of these,
Unjust, Satanic, futile, License laws.

This hue and cry, that Prohibition fails;
And cannot be enforced, is WHOLLY FALSE.
'Tis not a failure, but a grand success;
For undeniable statistics show:
Where Prohibition has been fairly tried,
It always has reduced, if not removed
The woe intoxicating drinks produce.
Of such statistics, one can find, with ease,
An almost endless host, to prove these facts,
If there were need: But this one point alone;
Forever most completely overthrows,
This cry of "failure" by the whisky "ring."
This point, a little child can understand.
If Prohibition fails so: We should like
To know; why, in the name of common sense,
All Liquor-dealers hate it as they do,
And fight it to the death, and rage and fume,
And curse and swear, and call its advocates
Fanatics, bigots, fools and hypocrites?
If they were honest (?) why did liquor-men
Send money, by the thousands, to the States
Of Kansas, Iowa and Maine, to fight

This so-called Prohibition "failure" there?
Do whiskey-men pour out their gold for naught?
Why have they pledged themselves, if 'tis required,
To furnish millions more to other States,
To fight "Amendments" pending everywhere,
"Prohibiting forever" their vile trade?
Do wise men fight an "utter failure" thus?
If Prohibition fails so, one would think
That liquor men would be the very first
To doff their hats and shout "*Hurrah!* HURRAH!
For Prohibition." "Oh! Consistency,
Thou art a jewel!" Oh! how fair thou art!
One is reminded by this "Liquor League"
Of that "good, pious grocer" who once said
To John, his boy: "John, have you chalked the starch?"
"Oh, yes," said John. "And did you put that sand
Into the sugar, John?" "I did," said John.
"And have you watered well that rum?" "I have,"
John said. "Well, then," said he, "COME IN TO PRAYERS."
Ah, no! These liquor-dealers know full well,
That of all foes the one they dread the most
Is Prohibition, "failure" though it be.
May God grant *many* "failures" such as this.

IV.

Well, "Prohibition INTERFERES," say they,
"WITH LIBERTY AND INDIVIDUAL RIGHTS."
It is affirmed "that all men have the right
To eat and drink and wear just what they please."
Hence "sumptuary laws" are all unjust.
Why, yes, of course, we have the right to eat
Or drink most deadly poisons, if we choose,
But if they kill us, need we be surprised?
Of course, all men and women have the right (?)
To run stark naked through our public streets.

Amid these cries for "liberty" we find
Beneath apparent fairness, deeply cloaked,
A fallacy which most men overlook,
And which the devil carefully conceals,
Lest, being seen, it might curtail his work
Of drafting new recruits for death and Hell,
By crippling his great growing liquor trade,
Which furnishes the most of these recruits.
This fallacy appears, when we reflect,
That Prohibition never says one word,
About what men must eat or drink or wear;
But only deals, with what they *make and sell.*
'Tis true, a state has no just right to say,
What men *must* eat, or what they *must not* drink:
Yet everywhere, all nations recognize
This principle, that states do have the right.
Not only to inspect, but to control
Completely, any thing their citizens,
May make or sell, or even give away,
Whenever it endangers public good,
Or brings about disaster to the State.
To-day we find, both Germany and France,
Prohibiting by law, the sale of pork,
Exported from our own America,
And none deny, their right to pass such laws.
And in our own beloved land, you see
This principle acknowledged everywhere:
No man can plant a powder magazine,
Or bone-dust factory, or slaughter-house,
Down in the hearts of cities or of towns;
Yet none complain of liberties curtailed.

Suppose some butcher, op'ning up his shop,
Begins to sell, diseased and tainted meat
Throughout your town, till many are made sick:
And furthermore, suppose you go to him,
And say, "See here Sir, you can't sell such meat;

It is against the law: What would you think,
If (like our bloated liquor men) he thrusts
Both thumbs into the arm-holes of his vest,
And "standing on his dignity" should say,
" This country's free: Men have a perfect right,
To eat and drink and wear, just what they please;
And therefore, I shall sell my tainted meat?"
What would you do? Why, if no other way
Could be devised, to stop his "horrid" trade,
Your town would gather round, that " dreadful" shop,
And taking out that "woful wicked" wretch,
You soon would hang him to the nearest tree;
While an admiring world, would say "Amen."
Now had we shops for selling tainted meat,
On every corner, and in every town
Throughout the land; they never could produce,
One-half the misery and crime and death,
Produced by all our soul-less liquor shops:
Yet (Oh! Consistency!) our Government
Prohibits, Yes, "PROHIBITS" that's the word,
Prohibits tainted meat and impure milk,
And "licenses" this deadly liquor trade;
Our greatest Curse; this deepest wrong of all;
This most stupendous evil of our age.
If this is liberty: Oh! let us hope,
That we, at least, may never be set free.
How can it injure "individual rights"
To stop this liquor traffic, anymore
Than stopping men from selling tainted meat,
Adulterated milk, or noxious food
Of any kind? Behold! how men sometimes,
Gulp down a camel, straining at a gnat!

Alas! there is a far more solemn side,
To this great question, touching " private rights,"
Which whisky men's consummate selfishness
Completely overlooks, and swooping down

It oft has blinded, thoughtless Temp'rance men.
These men misled, by sound instead of sense,
Have stupidly supposed, and still insist;
That States can pass no laws, which interfere
With citizens, who make and sell strong drink,
Without infringing on their liberties.
Oh! how one-sided, is this narrow view!
Have others then, no rights, in this free land,
But whisky "bloats" and "bonded liquor" lords?
These men, who deal out naught but pain and death?
These men, whose awful business, blasts the lives,
Of millions of their race; and sucks their souls
Down through the seething vortex of strong drink,
Into their hopeless Hell of endless woe;
Are there no "individual rights" but theirs?
And is there then, no liberty but rum's?
Where are the liberties of drunkard's wives?
The liberties of children, starved by drink?
The liberties of many noble men
Shot down with bullets fired by brandied brains?
What "individual rights" had that poor man,
Killed by a drunken madman, not long since,
Upon the railway, in a "sleeping" car
Of the "Ohio, Mississippi" road?
A man who has been drinking sev'ral days,
Is marching up and down, this sleeping car:
His brain seems like a mass of glowing coals
Almost white hot; At last the crisis comes:
All reason gone; his madness blazes forth
From blood-shot eyes: He draws his pistol out:
He whirls, and sends a bullet through the heart,
Of one, whom he had never seen before.
Had that dead man no "private liberties"
Or had his stricken wife and children none?

Again we ask: What of the liberties
Of LINCOLN; whose great name we all revere;

When just before, **Booth** killed him, it is known
He drank strong brandy, and thus nerved his arm
To slay our Nation's honored President?
Once more, with tearful eyes, and hearts yet sore,
From deep sad swelling aching grief, we ask:
What of the "individual liberties"
Of GARFIELD, our beloved martyred Chief;
When, just two days before the fatal shot,
His vile assassin had been "beastly" drunk?
Why, even in this *free*, FREE land of ours,
No one is safe, at any time or place,
From President to pauper, while this fiend
Of drink may freely range at liberty,
Destroying whom he will. Oh! brave and true
Americans! BEHOLD THE OTHER SIDE!
There is another side; and other rights
There are besides these so-called rights (?) of rum.
And other liberties besides those claimed
So loudly by the liquor-dealing ring.
May God soon open wide our blinded eyes,
To see, in what true liberty consists,
To wit: NO LIBERTY TO DO THE WRONG,
BUT UTMOST LIBERTY TO DO THE RIGHT.

V.

Again we hear these liquor men assert:
That "Prohibition STRIKES AT 'VESTED RIGHTS'
We have invested money in good faith,
In this great liquor traffic; and we claim,
That now the Government can pass no laws,
To stop this trade she has so long upheld;
For thus she sweeps away our source of wealth,
And renders valueless our property."
(How does this great objection harmonize,
With that one, claiming "Prohibition fails?"

He who tells one untruth, is oft compelled
To tell a second to conceal the first.)
There possibly may be some little weight (?)
In this objection, from the shameful fact.
That since her birth, our nation has sustained
And fostered, this great, growing, wicked trade,
And " legalized by law" this giant wrong.
But look a moment, at the other side.
We should remember this important truth:
That when some great and long-continued wrong
Is righted, then, must those concerned in it
Be injured, more or less; and as a rule
It hurts, those who are most to blame, the worst.
If men persist in doing what is wrong,
They must endure the whirlwind when it comes.
Suppose that " tainted-meat man" should affirm,
That he had put " his all " into that meat,
And would be ruined, if he could not sell:
All men would justly say: " We can't help that
Whatever happens, you sha'n't sell such meat."
It will be found, when Prohibition comes,
That it will come so slowly, all will have
The necessary time, to turn their wealth
Into some worthy, honest, useful trade.
Their money may not yield, quite such GREAT GAINS;
But what it does yield, will be clean and just,
Unstained by drunkards' wives and childrens' tears.
Such wealth will bless their homes, and give them peace.
Although they will not likely be so rich,
Yet much more happy will they be, than now
When all their wicked wealth is steeped in sin,
And crimsoned with the stains of human blood.

Some claim, "That if a state should stop this trade,
It should, at least, make good the loss of those
Engaging in this traffic, who would be
Thrown out of business, if a law was passed

Enacting Prohibition." Think you so ?
Why it would be more just, by far, to pay
For all the slaves set free, by our late war.
Behold! the ruin Drink has always wrought:
Behold! the countless millions, liquor men
Have stolen from the treasures of the State:
Behold! how they have trampled under foot
Our claims, and openly transgressed our laws:
Behoid! the great expense, their crimes entailed,
Behold! the little pittance, they have paid,
Toward meeting this expense; and all must see,
There's nothing in these claims, for "vested rights"
And that these men have caused enough of woe;
And made enough, out of their wicked trade;
And have no further claims upon the State,
However much they squirm beneath her stroke,
By which she ends their business, *for all time.*
Did Liquor Dealers pay back to the State,
A tithe, of all they've stolen from her wealth;
Eternity itself, would scarcely give.
Them time, by hardest toil, to pay their debt:
While every child of God, with horror knows,
A whole eternity, of speechless woe,
Will *never*, NEVER pay their debt to God :
Unless, before their death, the Spirit's grace,
Shall bless their souls, and lead them to the Cross,
And work repentence in their stony hearts.
Poor, wicked, wretched ones; They need our prayers.
God knows! 'Tis all the debt, to them, we owe.

Some people ask, apparently concerned,
" But then, WHAT WOULD WE DO WITH ALL OUR CORN,
If Prohibition should be made the law ?"
One good old lady says; "Make starch of it,
To stiffen the back-bones of Temp'rance men."
Perhaps the best reply of all was made
By one plain " Hoosier" farmer' not long since;

" Why, we will raise more pork—LESS HELL," he said.
Far better, let our grain rot in the fields:
Far better, pour it out into the sea,
Than turn it into brandy, gin and beer,
To lead ourselves, and neighbors down to death,
Are there no drunkards' fam'lies, in the land,
Whose money, had it not been spent for drink,
Might well have purchased, all our extra grain ?
Away! with all such senseless sophistries:
As if we must destroy our happy homes,
And starve our children; beggar all our land,
And scatter ruin everywhere; and bring
Down on us endless woes; and all to help
The Devil's liquor trade, for fear, forsooth,
We might not find a market for our grain!
Alas! Alas! All fools are not yet dead!

VI.

Again, some say: " THE BIBLE FAVORS DRINK,
And therefore, it is wrong to stop this trade.
Our Lord made wine, and doubtless drank it too;
Of course it cannot then, be wrong to drink.
All men, except a few religious cranks,
Reject this 'two-wine' theory, as false.
Oh! yes, my pious friend, we have you now;
The Bible's on our side; why, don't you know,
That Paul himself, told Timothy to take
A little wine, just for his stomach's sake ?
And don't you know, that almost everywhere
Throughout His Word, the great God blesses wine ?
Why then oppose what God himself commends ?"

We say. It is a most noteworthy fact:
That now, for ages, when some great reform
Has come, to help the world, and bless our race,

The Bible, first of all, is made to prove,
That this reform is wrong, and can't succeed.
How was it less than thirty years ago,
Here in our own beloved, favored land ?
Whole millions, then believed and proved, they thought,
From God's own Word: that Slavery was right.
Who tries to prove it from the Bible now ?
The time will come, and at no distant day,
When men will no more, think of bringing forth
The Bible, to uphold this liquor trade,
Than now they think, of making it support,
That vile "slave system," wiped out with our blood.
But does the Bible really favor rum ?

To this we firmly hold. God's Word is true;
And every word of it by Him inspired.
It follows then, if we accept this truth;
That God (unless He contradicts Himself;
Which every Christian knows, can never be)
Must be opposed to this great drunkard trade,
For in His holy word He plainly states:
" No drunkard can into my kingdom come."
And yet, we know, He longs that all be saved.
But that INTOXICATING wine was made
At Cana, by our Lord, we must deny;
And we defy, all men, or ANY MAN,
To PROVE, He EVER made or used such wine.
Our Lord was sinless, then, can we suppose,
That, at "that marriage," when the guests had drank
Already, much "poor wine," the Lord would make,
Much more, still stronger wine, to make them drunk ?
Since God is true: We know, it can not be,
That, that "strong drink" He curses, is the same,
With that "new wine" on which His blessing rests.
And is it not at least significant;
That when our blessed Savior, institutes
His "holy supper" just before His death,

Which is to be observed, throughout all time;
He does not even deign to speak of wine,
Nor once to mention it. He simply says,
" The cup" or else, perchance "fruit of the vine."
And as for Timothy, so rigid was
His total abstinence, that it required
A "God inspired command," before he would
Consent to take wine as a medicine,
Then JUST A LITTLE, for his stomach's sake.
We do believe there are two kinds of wine,
Concerning which, God in His Bible speaks:
The one fermented, and the other not;
One kind He blessed, the other kind He cursed:
And the presumption, we are bold to say,
Is VERY STRONG (and none can PROVE it false)
That never did our sinless Savior make,
Or use, fermented wines of any kind.
And Oh! that christian churches, would unite,
To banish from the "supper of their Lord"
The Devil's own "intoxicating bowl"
And only use the fresh "fruit of the vine"
Which never leads those who have once "reformed"
To seek, again, the drunkard's life of sin.

But on the other hand, suppose we grant,
, (And barely (?) possibly it may be so)
That Jesus, made and used, fermented wine:
It does not therefore follow, that our Lord,
Looks down upon our PRESENT liquor curse
Approvingly. Think you that Tender One
Who while on Earth, "broke never once
The bruised reed, nor quenched the smoking flax,"
Whose one great loving mission, was "to bind
Up broken hearts, and comfort those who mourn,"
Delights in this accursed liquor trade?
If He were here upon our Earth to-day,
And we should ask Him: Lord, dost thou approve

Of this great whisky trade, which everywhere,
Is spreading woe and ruin in its wake?
What answer would he make, do you suppose?
If He denounced the Pharisees, as thieves
And hypocrites; Think you, that He would speak
In tones more tender, to these men, who deal
Out death and Hell; against His strict command,
"Put not the bottle, to thy neighbor's lips?"
No Jesus favors not this awful curse;
His Bible stands, and will forever stand,
Opposed to this whole traffic in strong drink:
And time will vindicate, its changeless Truth,
However much, men now may wrest its words
And twist them round to serve the Devil's ends.
"The Heavens and the Earth, shall pass away;
But never shall one jot of God's Word fail."
And this unchanging Word, distinctly says:
The drunkard's life is woe; his death is Hell.

How foolish then, it is for men to urge,
That God Himself and His most holy Word,
Approve, our present, blighting, liquor curse.
Let us remember, that the times have changed:
That this adulterated and distilled,
This "doctored," poisoned, and fermented stuff,
Called "liquor" by us now, is nothing like
The mild and grape-made wines of Bible times.
'Tis only, in the last few hundred years,
The Devil has discovered, to our race,
These deadly drugs, fermented and distilled;
But as he grows more versed and bold in sin,
He uses these dread liquors, more and more,
Until to-day, his whole dominion shakes,
With shouts and praises of this Demon Drink;
Who drags one soul each minute, down to death;
No wonder Satan grins, with hellish glee,
And counts this most infernal Fiend of all,

His greatest Agent, in his work of woe.
Think you, that God did not fore-know all this,
Nor had it in His mind, when in His Word,
He lays down this great Truth. It is most good,
" To DRINK NO WINE, *or anything*, WHEREBY
THY BROTHER IS OFFENDED, OR MADE WEAK."
Let infidels and skeptics sneer and scoff,
And rage against the Scriptures, if they wish;
But henceforth, let no true believer say:
That God's most holy Bible favors Drink.

VII.

Again, these whisky men, with tearful (?) eyes,
Inform us, " That OUR GREATEST REVENUES
COME FROM THEIR TRAFFIC, and our Government.
Could never be maintained, were these cut off."
What an objection!!! Are we then so poor
That National expenses, can't be met,
Unless we enter into partnership,
With this foul Demon Drink, our greatest curse,
And foster and uphold our greatest foe ?
Must our expenses as a Government,
Be always settled, with the price of blood?
Must we continue evermore to reap,
Our largest revenues, from haunts of vice,
From poverty and pain, from sin and shame?
Far better, trust the people to defray
The national expense, or better still,
Impose a tax, to raise our revenues,
Directly on the people. They would find
It easier by far, to pay such tax,
Than to maintain, this wasteful liquor trade.
Just give us half the money, spent for rum,
And we could pay all national and state,
All county and municipal expense;

And then besides, sweep from our nation's books,
Our public debt, in less that five short years.

Here is one fact, men often overlook:
There reigns on High, a just and holy God,
Who "keeps the books" by which all men and states
Are judged. Now as to individual men,
There is a future world to judge them in,
Where crooked things of Earth, are all made straight:
The Righteous there are blessed, who suffered here;
And wicked ones, who while on Earth, seemed blest
Must meet their punishment, beyond the tomb.
Not so with nations. They are judged on Earth.
They have no place on High: so when they sin,
They suffer here; for God who changes not,
Has said. "If nations do transgress my laws,
And walk not in my ways; I'll visit then
Their faults with rods, their sins with chastisements."
Because, on High, a just God kept the books,
The proudest nations, Earth has ever known,
Have crumbled into dust: and all their pomp,
And wealth and might, have long since passed away.
Nor need we think, that this our goodly land,
Shall never share a like disastrous fate.
If we neglect to heed the warning voice,
Of Him, who keeps the records from on High.
Already have we felt, the heavy hand
Of God in anger, for our nation's sin.

Was it an accident that LINCOLN died?
Upon the eighth of April, "sixty-five,"
The Southern forces, under Gen'ral Lee,
Surrendered to the forces under Grant,
At Appomatox Court-House; by which act
The war was virtually brought to a close.
'Twas Saturday; and during all that night.
The busy wires, were sending far and near,

Throughout the Northern States, the joyous news
The holy Sabbath morn, dawned; bright with Peace,
And seemed to say, to one and all: " Thank God,
Come, seek His "courts" and worship at His feet."
But people everywhere, seemed wild with joy;
And in our cities and our larger towns,
Instead of going to the "house of prayer"
And praising God; for Victory and Peace;
They rushed "pell-mell" into the public streets,
Fired cannons; and sang patriotic songs;
Made speeches; and in many other ways,
Dishonored God's most sacred day of rest.
The hearts of many of God's children bled,
To see this wholesale disregard, for Him
And for His holy day; and some true souls,
Predicted, that in Justice, He would bring,
Some dire calamity, upon our land,
For this bold desecration of His day.
Was this a prophecy? Mark well, this fact.
The sounds of these wild Sabbath revelries,
Had scarcely died away: When Friday night,
The Fourteenth-day of April; Hark! Behold!
All stand aghast! for all have heard the crack
Of the assassin's pistol: and our Chief,
Lies dying in our nation's Capitol.
One Sabbath in the wildness of our joy,
We trample under-foot, God's holy day;
The next, we sit and weep in silence, dumb,
With stricken hearts, around the lifeless form
Of our slaughtered Chieftain. Oh! we ask
Once more, in view of all these solemn facts;
Was it an accident, that Lincoln died?

Thou, great Republic! Proud, United States!
Oh! tremble, for thy princely revenues!
They largely come from crime and woe and death:
Thy liquor gold, is stained with thine own blood:

Each whisky dollar, tells a tale of want:
Each dime is wet with thine own children's tears,
Wrung from thy drunkard's wives and starving babes.
How canst thou touch, a single-blood-stained cent
Drained from the Godless gains, of this vile trade?
Oh! Proud and Rich Republic! Bear in mind,
That God is just; and that He keeps thy books! !!

How was it, just a few short years ago?
Our Southern brethren, thinking they were right,
(But were in error sadly) boasted much,
That "labor, in the South was free.   They kept
Their slaves, and paid them nothing for their work."
Our nation sanctioned that accursed, wrong
And how it ended: Ah! we know too well!
God kept the books; and by our awful war,
We paid, for every dollar, every cent,
Of that "free labor" with the precious blood,
Of husbands, fathers, brothers, lovers, sons,
Who died, to strike the shackles from the slave.
On High, that same just God, still keeps the books;
And for each blood-stained dime and dollar drained,
From this, still more crime–crimsoned, liquor Curse,
He will, in due time, call us to account.
Why was our noble GARFIELD slain? And why
Are earthquakes, cyclones, fires and floods so rife?
Oh! let us hear and heed, God's warning voice,
And cease depending, for our revenues,
Upon the Devil's traffic in strong drink;
Lest, God's hot thunder-bolts, of long pent wrath.
Blast us forever, and His angry waves
Of fury, dashing o'er our rum-cursed land
Engulf us, in this maelstrom of strong drink,
And sink us into ruin, for our sin.
Must we destroy, the bodies and the souls,
Of thousands of our people, every year,
To raise the funds, to run the Government?

Well may we hide our heads, with burning **shame**;
For **we are** paying off our public debt,
With revenues, of liquor's blood-stained gold.
Well may we tremble, for our future fate,
Unless repenting, ere it is too late,
We stop, henceforth, all partnership with Drink;
Lest God who keeps **our** nation's books, should come,
And should requite us, "double for **our** sin."

VIII.

" WE DON'T ENFORCE," say they, "THE LAWS WE HAVE,
How then shall we enforce a stricter law?"
Of course, we don't enforce the laws we have,
And Never can, for they **are** wicked laws,
And wicked law, can **never** be enforced.
Behold! our laws for "fugitives" who fled
From Southern Slavery, to Northern soil:
That law; which seized these slaves, and sent them back,
To groan, beneath a bondage, **worse than** death.
Was that most wicked law **enforced?**
So from the very nature of the **case,**
These wicked License laws, will never be
Enforced: FOR GOOD MEN CAN'T AND BAD MEN WON'T.
'Tis vain; to set a thief, to watch a thief.
Like "Pat," who stole the pig, but was discharged
When clearly he was guilty. "Ah!" said Pat,
" And faith, I knowed, I wud be innocint,
For did not sivin, of **them** jury-min,
Have aich a paice, uv **that** same blessed pig?"
How can it then be strange, that whisky laws,
Enacted and upheld by liquor men,
Should fail, to stem the tide of drunkenness?
Let any Temp'rance **man,** go **into** "court,"
And **try** to make **these laws,** suppress strong **drink;**
He **fails,** he always has, and always will;

Not only are these **laws all wrong, but** more;
In almost every county-seat, **and state,**
Our "courts" and "legislatures" **are** controlled,
By this vile liquor **trade, to** which **they** bow,
And at whose "beck **and rod"** they speak and act.
Just look behind the scenes, and you will **see,**
Why courts and legislatures, bend to **rum,**
The **most** of them, are fishing for the "spoils;"
And "Rummies" fill their greedy hands with gold.
But more; these "Rummies" go to them and say:
" Our votes elected you; therefore you must,
  Submit to us, cr we will "cut your throats
  Politic'ly." **AND AS A RULE THEY YIELD.**
  (No wonder Temp'rance work "goes **by the** board.")
  This game of "buy and sell" is going **on**
  Between our Office Seekers every day,
  And liquor men, **and has been, now** for years.
  Thus have good **Temp'rance men** been duped; and **laws**
  (Through which, **the "Liquorites" could** always find,
  Some loop-hole to escape by) **have** been passed;
  Our legislatures, bribed **by whisky** gold;
  Our Office Holders, bought **by whisky votes,**
  Have passed such laws, to "hold **the Temp'rance men;"**
  And yet, have whispered to the "Liquor League"
" We merely **want** to hold the Temp'rance **vote;**
  But you may rest assured, these license laws
  Can never be, and *shall* not be enforced,
  At least, so long as *we* shall **have** control."

Oh! Temp'rance **men! Have WE NO RIGHTS? No VOTES?**
Must we submit, to this accursed scheme,
To cheat us out of all we hold most **dear?**
Awake! all honest, noble, Temp'rance men!
And let us stand up bravely, **for our** rights.
We have our rights; **what ever "Rummies" say:**
We have a voice and vote, let us be bold;
To use them for our country and our God.

We have been far too easy, in the past.
We need more stamina, more real back-bone.
We need to let these "Rummies" understand,
They *shall not* rule and ruin, this fair land.
We too, must go to those who make our laws,
And say to them: "*Our* votes elected you:
So you must take out of our "statute" books,
These wicked laws, which can not be enforced,
And give us laws which WILL remove this curse:
And if you will not do what we demand;
We'll turn you out, and put in those who will.
A large majority is on our side,
If we would only all together stand,
And heart to heart, work for our common cause.
A county, is "ground down" by twenty men;
A mighty city, often crushed and cursed,
It may be, by one thousand Liquorites:
Our whole great nation, fifty millions strong,
Is groaning, underneath the iron heel
Of HALF A MILLION, licensed "Liquor Lords."

Oh! Temp'rance Workers! Come, Awake! Arise!
God's on our side, and Right is on our side;
Let us stand firm! Let us be brave and true!
And soon we'll see the turning of the tide;
And when at length it turns, and our vote
Outweighs the whisky vote; we'll see these men
Who now are cringing at the feet of rum,
Turn 'round, and shout, "I am a Temp'rance man,
My mother taught me Temp'rance from a child."
And for our votes, they will denounce strong drink
As fiercely, as they now proclaim its praise.
And when the battle, has at last been fought;
The vict'ry won; the Demon Drink laid low;
Then who will get the credit, for the fight?
Will those brave men, who by their votes, compelled
Their legislators, to enact just laws;

And made these Office Seekers, change their minds?
No, No, indeed! Ah! No! but these same men
Who now are aiding rum; will then stand forth,
In all their dignity, and boundless ''brass"
And shout, with one accord: "WE KILLED THE BEAR!"
'Twas always thus, in every great Reform.

IX.

Again they tell us, "It is better far,
To have no law at all; than have a law
Which cannot be enforced." "We have," say they,
" Upon our statute books, enough of laws
Already, if they only were enforced,
To quickly, stamp this liquor business out."
Oh, blinded Leaders, of the still more blind!
If these profound objections, show your minds,
When, YE once die, all wisdom will be dead.
" Enough of Temp'rance laws?" Why, Yes, indeed!
We have enough; that's true: SUCH AS THEY ARE;
AND FAR TOO MANY, FOR OUR COUNTRY'S GOOD.
" Enforce these "wicked" laws?" As well attempt,
With one small cup, to dip the ocean dry.

Once more, we hear these Liquor Dealers say:
" If PEOPLE only would enforce these laws,
There would be little trouble, with this trade."
Who rule this land; and who are sov'reign here?
The people? or the men who execute
The people's will? Must we indeed elect
Our Officers, to do our nation's work,
And then have all this work to do ourselves?
Whose business is it, to enforce the law?
The people's? or those Officers, who are
Elected, with that very end in view?
Our Officers, should serve the people's will;

Whereas too often now, we are their dupes.
They make us wicked laws, and then sit down,
And tell us to enforce them, if we can.
And if we do attempt it; they arise
And say, " The Constitution's in the way,"
Or by some other pretext, just as false,
They manage to give whisky men full **sway.**
Instead of telling these—our "public" men,
Just what we want; and what we *mean to have;*
Year after **year, we** vote for liquor men,
And then **bow** down on bended knees, and **beg**
These men to do their duty.   Oh! for shame!
Let us no longer, vote for Liquorites,
And **then** *"petition"* them **to stop** their trade:
But let us be more **wise, and vote** for none,
Who are not "pledged" to execute our will.
They are our servants; and to get our votes,
Will gladly **hear and** heed, our just demands,
When once, our votes outnumber, those of rum.

These Dear, Consistent, Liquor-dealing Knaves;
Are very much concerned, just now, for fear;
" If we should pass a Prohibition law,
It could not be enforced; and this would have
A bad effect on people everywhere,
By teaching them to disregard all law,
Till anarchy, at last, would seal our doom."
" Oh! better far," say they, "to have no law;
Than have one, to be trampled under foot."
Ye, Patriotic, Noble-minded men!
How often, will your wisdom save the State?
Oh, how ye tremble, at the awful thought,
That laws enacted, might not be enforced!
Oh, ye who daily break the laws we have,
Whence springs this sudden **loyalty** to law?
When into Kansas, Prohibition came:
Oh, how **you bloated,** blear-eyed drunkards_wept,

(Who had not been to church for twenty years)
To think, that should this "awful law" prevail,
The Church, would not be able to obtain
" Communion wine" AND ALL MEN WOULD "BE LOST."
And when, to comfort them, a good old man
Suggested, they could use, some "raisin juice"
One poor old "beer-bloat" tearfully replied;
" Well Deacon, you may possibly palm off
Your raisin-water, on your fellow-men;
But you can not deceive the blessed Lord:"
And that poor fellow, trembled at the thought,
That Prohibition, would destroy the Church.
Whence sprang that sudden zeal, for Christian work?

But coming back, directly to the plea,
" That Prohibition, could not be enforced,
And would create a disrespect for law."
We ask, Do these same liquor men, who fear,
" If passed, a Prohibition law would fail"
Respect, these so-called Temp'rance laws we have ?
There is not one saloon, in all this land,
That does not violate existing laws.
Why, in collecting liquor revenues,
The government must watch these whisky men
Just like it would, a set of thieving Knaves:
For every chance they get, they break the law,
And mock at "Justice" in their dreadful work.
And yet these very men, turn round and cry,
" No law, is better than a law that's dead:
Oh, don't, don't pass a Prohibition law,
For it will fail, and thus disgrace the land."
Oh! Precious Jewel! Sweet Consistency !
In Liquor's galaxy, how bright thou art !!?

The history of nation's, makes this plain:
That holy laws, ennoble men and states;
And lead to happiness and strength and peace.

Though sometimes broken, yet they win respect;
And as they are enforced, they lift men up,
To higher aims, and better views of life.
While it is just as true, that wicked laws,
Degrade all those, who make them, or attempt
To put them into practice. Everywhere
They are despised. They lead men into sin,
And end in being trampled under-foot.
Their tendency, from first to last, is bad.
They lead to misery, sometimes to blood;
And always cause a jubilee in Hell.

To shun the bad, is wise; to choose the good,
Is wiser still; hence every righteous law,
Enacted and enforced, confirms, supports,
All other righteous laws; and all combine,
To make it harder, to commit a crime;
And ever easier, to do what's right.
'Tis true; men often break these righteous laws;
But must they, therefore, straightway be repealed?
We have our laws, against all other crimes;
As treason, murder, bribery and theft;
And yet men steal, and kill their fellow men:
Must we enact no laws against these crimes,
For fear, they might be broken now and then?
Had we a righteous Prohibition law,
It would be just as rigidly enforced,
And would as fully check, the crime of drink;
As laws for treasons, murders, bribes and thefts,
Restrain mankind, from these obnoxious crimes.
Does Prohibition fail, because, perchance,
It can't stop "drinking" everywhere, at once?
As well assert; all murder laws are vain,
Because, sometimes, man slays his brother man.

While wicked laws, blast all respect for law,
A righteous law upholds, all righteous laws;

For in proportion, as it is enforced,
It strengthens, the enforcement of all law.
Suppose "all drinking" could be stopped at once;
The law for murder, soon would feel the change;
For nearly all our murders spring from Drink.
Would not the law for theft, be strengthened, too?
Where can you find a greater thief than rum?
And what about the law for bribery?
Who can afford, to offer larger bribes
Than these poor blinded, wretched whisky men,
Whom Satan hires, to help replenish Hell?
And what about the laws of chastity?
Would they not also be more strictly kept?
Well does wine's color mark the harlot's house;
For wine produces lusts, and these in turn
Beget vile fornications; yea, and worse,
Adulteries, with all their nameless woes.
Oh, where in all the catalogue of laws
Enacted to suppress the blackest crimes,
Is ONE, that Prohibition will not aid?

Thou All-wise God! Thou art THE SOURCE OF LAW
Both natural and moral. Born of Thee
All laws together work to do Thy will,
And at thy bidding execute those plans
Which glorify Thy name, and bless mankind.
Help us then Lord! to bring our human laws
Into conformity to Thine and thus
Obtain Thy blessing, and avoid Thy curse.

Great numbers think, that in these Gospel days,
There is no need for law. "We are" say they,
" No longer under law, but under grace."
'Tis true, we're under grace, but 'tis not true,
That we are not amenable to law.
For Christ Himself declared; "If ye love Me
Keep My commandments." No! God's holy law

Is still in force, **and** men **are** being brought
Each moment, more and **more** beneath its sway.
The World's not growing worse, by any means,
But one by one, man's laws, **are** being made,
In sweet accord, to harmonize with **God's.**

In Revelation we are plainly told,
" An Angel with a great chain in his hand
Comes down from Heav'n to Earth, and laying hold,
On **that** old Dragon-Serpent, who is called
The Devil, binds him **for a** thousand years."
This chain **the Angel uses,** probably IS LAW.
And with it, **even now, for** aught we know,
'Tis likely he is binding Satan fast.
Just **as the** spider's **victim, strand** by **strand,**
Is bound up in the **meshes of** her web;
Just so, God's mighty Angel, link by link,
And fold by fold, is wrapping Satan round
With that great breakless chain which **we call law.**
Each time the Angel **wraps** another coil
Around his slimy victim, it curtails
To some **extent, his** power to destroy.
When Slavery went down, the Angel **wrapped**
A mighty coil around **our** fiendish foe;
And when the Liquor-Traffic **bites the dust**
A still more mighty band, **will** girdle him:
Till one by one, the chain's coils all complete,
The mighty Angel lifting him aloft,
Bound hand and foot, shall hurl him into **Hell,**
Amid **the glad** refrain of holy hosts,
Who sweetly **sing, "The** kingdoms **of** this World
Have now become the kingdoms of our **Lord,"**
Our great Arch-Enemy is overcome;
Now Truth and Mercy meet, **and** Righteousness
And Peace have sweetly kissed: **Truth** springs from Earth,
And Righteousness once **more** looks down from Heav'n,
FOR HUMAN LAW AND **LAW** DIVINE ARE ONE."

X.

And last of all, but by no means, the least;
They tell us, "Prohibition will effect,
And *interfere with "Politics,"* Perhaps,
DISTURB THE TWO GREAT "PARTIES" in the land."
Of course it will; but pray, what matters that?
It has already entered "Politics:"
The liquor men themselves, have placed it there:
They have declared, not once, but *many* times,
In their Conventions, "We will NEVER vote,
For any man, for any office small or great;
For any "PARTY" National or State;
That shall, in any way, for any cause,
Regard with favor "Prohibition laws."
And late elections show, that whisky men
All vote (not as they pray?) but as they "swear."

We ask again, What if this question should,
Effect the "two great (?) Parties" of our land?
This giant curse of Drink is National:
Is not its cure then, National as well?
The issue MUST be forced: Then we can have
A fair discussion, of the "rights and wrongs"
Of this great question. That is what we want;
And what we mean to have, ere many days.
God's time has come; and this great question can
No LONGER BE IGNORED. The patient hosts
Of Temp'rance men, have been, not only duped,
But basely disappointed, LONG ENOUGH,
By "Party promises" not ONCE FULFILLED,
How do these two great parties stand to-day
On this, THE GREATEST QUESTION OF THE AGE?
As much as possible, they BOTH IGNORE
The truth of Prohibition; and contend;
For what? For some great Principle of Right?

Ah! no! for "spoils." Their only motto is;
" To victors" (evermore) "belong the spoils."

There is not one great living issue, now
Between these two old Parties of to-day.
The "Party Leaders" strive to keep a "stir"
About the "Tariff" and the poor "Chinese,"
The "Mormons" and such minor things as these:
And then at last, fall back upon the War;
And resurrect and flaunt the "bloody shirt"
And thus keep up the semblance of a fight.
The questions; of the "Sov'reignty of States;"
Of "Slavery;" "Secession;" all are *dead*
And *buried*. Why not let them rest in peace?
Those questions have been settled, once for all;
Why not take up some problem, still unsolved?

In Politics, a "Party" is a means
To reach a given end; and *nothing more*:
And by the end proposed, we gauge its worth.
A Party that does right deserves support.
A Party that does wrong however fair
Its promises; however loud its boasts
Of what it has done, or expects to do;
Should not receive the votes of righteous men.
No! Never!. Let each honest upright man,
Put Truth above his Party. Principle
Above mere policy; and standing forth,
Upon the side of Right; be brave enough,
To leave his Party, when it goes astray,
And enters into partnership with crime,
And plunges, headlong, into open sin.

Too often men, and even Christian men,
Are wholly blinded, to their Party's faults.
They think, because, their Party has been right,
It always must be right; and hence, they vote

Their Party ticket "straight;" and where it leads
They follow blindly; stopping not to think,
That God will, one day, call them to account
For every vote, cast in behalf of sin,
By those who follow Party, right or WRONG.
'Tis true, in this free land; we learn to love
Our Parties much; but let us bear in mind,
That God and Right, Humanity and Truth,
Have claims, as much above, mere Party claims,
As Heaven is above our lowly Earth.

What makes a Party? Is it not composed
Of those who vote its ticket, and maintain
Its principles? But are they worthy men,
And seeking worthy ends? Then may we love
Our Party, and support it; but if not;
Let every honest Christian man beware,
Lest, he walk blindly, into Satan's snare.
Come, let us measure, by this righteous rule,
The two old Parties of our land to-day,
And see if they can safely stand the test.

The SETTLED POLICY, for many years,
Both Democratic and Republican,
Has been, to "license" this accursed Drink;
And thus to legalize, its countless woes.
Now "license" means: "Let beer and whisky flow."
Hence every "license Party" is in fact
A whisky Party. Therefore, EVERY MAN
Who casts his ballot, with the Democrats,
Or with Republicans; VOTES WHISKY STRAIGHT;
According as these Parties, stand to-day,
And has been doing so for sixteen years.
They both are bidding for the whisky vote:
One; boldly, openly, without a blush:
The Other; no less truly; yet pretends,
To foster Temp'rance, underneath her wings,

But while she shouts "Sobriety" she turns
And licks the dust beneath the feet of Rum,
And sells her "*sober*" voters to their foes.

There are good men, the very best of men
In both these Parties; but they ought to see
By this time, surely, that they don't control
Their Parties now, nor will they ever rule
In Parties, which have compromised with sin:
Much less effect in them, a true Reform,
While they (involved in common guilt) commit,
The very crimes, against which they contend.
Since this is true; 'tis vain to strive to change
These Parties, by remaining in their folds.
They both have grown amazingly corrupt;
And we must leave them, if we would effect,
The final overthrow of deadly Drink.

Oh, Christian Brethren! Do we love our homes?
Our wives and little ones? Our neighbors, friends?
Oh! Do we love our Country, great and free?
Aye, more; above all: Do we love our God?
Then let us join some Party, fully pledged,
To fight grim Rum, and drive him from the Earth.
Already this Grand Party, has been formed:
A Party fraught with precious destinies:
A Party undefiled, as yet, with "spoils:"
A Party small at present; but ere long
Her proud "Propeller" will be driving on,
Through "sober" seas the "grand old ship of state."
See!! Prohibition, waves upon her flag;
And Prohibition, is her battle cry;
Her name is Prohibition, and her voice
Peals out: for "God and Home and Native Land."
May God soon grant to her complete success.

XI.

But, very frequently, you hear it urged,
That "Prohibition's something, States alone
Should deal with; for the Government at large,
Has nothing in the question, "pro or con." "
Sometimes, our "wisest (?) statesmen" and " Plumed-
    Knights"
Affirm this truth (?) with "gravest gravity."
" This question's local; and it can not be
Made National." This is the old, old song.
Was Slavery not "local?" Was it not
Made National?" We ask who has control
Of our "District of Columbia?"
Of all our "Territories" great or small?
Does not our "Congress" have complete control
O'er all these places? Now suppose the States,
Could all be Prohibition States; and yet,
Our Congress, should remain composed, as now,
Of men who strongly favored Drink. Would not
Our Territories; and the sacred soil,
O'er which, our Nation's Capitol, now lifts
Its dome, and flings its shadow far and wide,
Be then, as deeply cursed with beer and rum
As they are now? And if our Congress chose,
To manufacture liquors by the ton,
In all those places, and should ship them round
Throughout our Prohibition States: We ask,
As things now stand; who could resist its will?
Some point us to the States of Kansas, Maine,
And Iowa, and say; "See! in those States
They carried Prohibition, yet, they did
Not take the question, into "Politics."

We answer, First: Suppose this should be done;
And one by one, the other States, should come,

And take their stand, beside those three grand States:
All men can see, that in a little while,
Our "Union" would be rent; for we would have,
Here; "Prohibition States" there; "Whisky States"
And as our martyred Lincoln truly said:
" This nation cannot live HALF-SLAVE, HALF-FREE."
So just as truly, our gallant Chief,
The brave and noble, good and true "St. John,"
Has said: "Our Nation cannot live, HALF-DRUNK,
HALF-SOBER." Slav'ry's war, is warning us,
That just so sure, as like produces like;
Unless we make this question National
At once; ere long, our "Union" will be rent
Asunder, by another civil war,
And brother will meet brother, once again,
Upon the field of battle, face to face,
And bathe their hands, in one another's blood.

We answer Second: That the statement's false:
In these three States, they did not, could not keep,
The question wholly out of Politics.
The people, rising in their might, compelled
The Party, then in power, to submit
The question, for their votes; although it was
Decidedly against, its honest wish.
Again those States have found, and will still find,
Their hardest fight, is to enforce the law.
And they will soon find out, that they must have,
A "Prohibition Party" in their midst,
Before they can obtain complete success.
For BOTH old Parties, just as in the past,
Will "sell out" Prohibition, WHEN THEY CAN.

We answer, Third: That many States, could not
Get Prohibition, in a thousand years,
If States must grapple with Strong Drink alone.
When would these California vine-clad hills,

Be wholly free, from rum's heart-rending wrongs,
So long as our Legislature scoffs,
At God, and at his Sabbath; then goes wild
In boastings, over California's wines?

For Prohibition to succeed, it must
Be in the Constitution of the State.
For "statutory Prohibition" is
And always must be, very insecure.
Now if a Legislature is composed
Of men, from Parties, which are both opposed
To Prohibition: Can you ever get
The question to the people? Talk of "fraud"
Among the Negro voters of the South!!!
For instance; take Ohio, in the North!!
How have the "Grand Old Parties" treated her,
While seeking to be freed from Liquor's curse?
For thirty years, her Constitution has
Refused to "license" rum: yet all this time,
When there was not one thing, to hinder them
From passing stringent Prohibition laws;
Republicans, and Democrats alike,
Agreed, that "to refuse to license" meant,
" Free Whisky" everywhere. Thus, all these years,
They trampled down, Ohio's Temp'rance men,
" And when they asked for bread; they got a stone."
" Petitions thick as hail" rained on the heads
Of Legislators. But 'twas all in vain.

At last these patient hosts grew desperate.
Republicans were ruling. Temp'rance men
Demanding freedom from the curse of Drink,
Began to leave the Party, which so long
Had failed completely, to redress their wrongs.
The "Party Leaders" soon became alarmed;
They saw that something must be done, at once;
Or suffer sure defeat. What did they do?

In order to appease the liquor men;
They First, submitted, for the People's votes,
A vile "Amendment" LICENSING Strong Drink.
Which TWICE before the People had refused:
And voted down by large majorities.
Then after that; they did at last, submit
" Amendment Number TWO!" Which was a fair
And just "Amendment" to prohibit Drink.
What did those "Grand Old (Whisky) Parties" do?
The Democratic Leaders, to a man,
All fought, "Amendment Number Two" of course.
But what about the "Grand Republicans ?"
Did they espouse "Amendment Number Two ?"
Oh, No ! they also sought the Whisky vote.
Hence all their Leaders, lauded to the skies,
" Amendment Number ONE" while everywhere,
They fiercely fought "Amendment Number TWO."
Although these two old Parties thus combined
To slaughter Prohibition; yet, Thank God !
Good old Ohio's noble Christian men
Were not all blind. They rose, and proudly spurned
" Amendment Number One" beneath their feet;
But **carried,** by an overwhelming vote,
" Amendment Number TWO." Alas ! Alas !
'Twas all in vain. The "Grand (?) Old Parties" met;
And counting out the votes to suit themselves,
Declared "Amendment Number TWO" was LOST.
This fact, no one as yet has dared deny;
But it has been the Liquor-dealers' boast,
That thus they "counted out," the Temp'rance vote.
What "Southern frauds" compare with that ?
What State can carry Prohibition then,
So long as BOTH "old Parties," thus combine,
To "pool their issues" and "to count it out ?"

It will be found as Time and Truth advance;
And as THE COMING CONFLICT fiercer grows;

That very few, if any, more great States,
Will carry Prohibition; till they cease
To look to these "old Parties" IN THE LEAST,
But everywhere, proceed at once, to form
A Prohibition Party, WHOLLY PLEDGED
To free the People from the Curse of Rum.

We answer, Fourth: Our Government is NOT,
A mere "Confederation" of loose States.
We are a "Union" in the truest sense:
If Prohibition is so good for one,
It must be good for half, yea ALL the States,
And for the whole United States,
Aye, for our rum-cursed race, throughout the World.
How can we reach those States, where Liquor reigns
And always will; if they are left to fight,
This dreadful, deadly Demon, all alone?
Thank God ! There is one way it can be done.
It must be by some party under God,
Which stands committed to this blessed work.
Then everywhere, along this line, in States
And Territories; let true Temp'rance men
Of every race, all pray and work and vote:
In every State make Prohibition ring;
And place it, just as soon as possible,
Within the "Constitution" of the State.
Elect a "Congress" which will soon submit
A National Amendment, to the States,
Prohibiting Strong Drink, forevermore,
From all our Nation, and from all her lands.
And when at last, "Three-fourths of all the States"
Shall stand forth freed from Liquor's galling curse,
We'll proudly write upon our Nation's flag,
And still more proudly write it, large and deep
Upon the "Constitution of our land,
ETERNAL PROHIBITION EVERYWHERE,
FROM EVERYTHING THAT SHALL INTOXICATE.

This is the only way, those "Whisky" States,
Which otherwise, must evermore be cursed,
Can all be freed forever, from Strong Drink.
Will all this be accomplished, in one day ?
Or without "organized" persistent toil ?
Those who so glibly talk, of working up
This wondrous Prohibition Cause, without
A Prohibition Party in the field,
Forget the other side, the "whisky" side;
And what fierce opposition must be met.
The Liquor men, are strong in wealth and votes,
And will fight Prohibi.ion to the last:
Hence, if they have "BOTH PARTIES" on their side;
And if the Prohibitionists have NONE;
The "Liquorites" must always win the day.
From all these reasons, is it not quite clear,
That if the Prohibition Cause succeeds,
A Prohibition Party, is required ?

XII.

Again, they say, "These Prohibitionists
Are all "Fanatics" and of course, will fail:
Poor things ! They mean well; but Alas ! what fools !
To think THEIR "Little Party" shall succeed,
And triumph over all its mighty foes."
Oh ! Brother Prohibitionists ! Stand firm.
" ONE MAN, if GOD is only ON HIS SIDE;
Has evermore, A GRAND MAJORITY."

If God be for us; WHO can lay us low ?
We may be called "Fanatics" but in this,
We fare no worse, than have the BEST of earth.
The Prophets and Apostles; holy men
Of every age; great men of every grade;
Reformers: Luther, Calvin, Zwingle, Knox;
Brave Missionaries, fearless Ministers,

Like Whitefield, Westley, Martyn and McCheyne.
Likewise Lloyd Garrison, and poor John Brown;
A Lincoln, and a Sumner; all were called,
" Fanatics." Yea, still more than all of these;
The Blessed Saviour, of our sin-cursed World;
The Mighty God; Creator; Lord of all;
In whom all Wisdom dwelt: He too, was called,
Fanatic, said to be "beside Himself."
The greatest fools, may call the wisest men,
" Fanatics." Does that really make them so?
If those true noble men who advocate,
The Prohibition, of our greatest Curse
Are all "Fanatics Would that *many more*
Of such FANATICS; might *beset* our Land.

Profoundest wisdom (from a liquor view)
Once more, informs us "That we can't succeed;
Because we build our "Platform on ONE plank."
The Prohibition Party fails; because
It "rides a hobby" and sees nothing else."
To this we answer. Nations are like men;
Success or failure, come to them alike,
According to the same unchanging laws.
You never see, a wise man, undertake
To do a dozen mighty deeds, at once;
But one by one, he takes up each hard task,
And ends the First, before the next begins,
Until at last, he finishes them all.
The wise Commander, knows it will not do
To undertake, at once, to capture all
The breast-works, thrown around a well-manned Fort:
But one by one, he storms them till they fall.
Just so with nations, and the hosts of Truth:
They can not triumph over Satan in a day;
Nor silence all his guns of war at once:
But one by one, they beat his ramparts down,
Until they hurl him from his throne, at last;
And God consigns him to eternal woe.

All great Reforms, from small beginnings rise.
Christianity itself, so small at first,
Now blazes into every land on Earth,
Behold! "The Reformation" at it's birth!
A few brave men, opposed on every side,
Stood firmly for this Truth; "Man saved by grace,
Is justified by faith in Jesus Christ;"
And with this glorious doctrine, shook the World.
Thus every Great Reform, mankind has seen,
Was always grounded on, some ONE grand Truth
And first defended, by a few brave men;
Who knowing they were right, would rather die
At any time, than for the sake of life,
Deny the principles, they had espoused:
Around this small, but faithful earnest band,
Still other noble souls, would take their stand
Till that great Truth, at last, would sweep the land.

What has the history of "Parties" been,
Since first our free Republic, had its birth;
Or farther still; since first our fathers stood,
Upon the shores of this fair land, and breathed
The air of liberty? 'Tis evermore
The same old story. Some gigantic wrong,
Is forced upon the People; till at last,
It can be borne no longer; then they rise
Led to the conflict, by a few brave souls,
Who in their righteous indignation, dare
To plant themselves, upon their "sov'reign rights,"
And boldly "beard the lion in his den."
Defending some great moral truth, these men,
Though few at first, would shout the battle cry,
And others soon would 'round their standard flock,
Until resistless Truth, would win the day,
And vindicate the cause of those oppressed.

Our glorious "Revolutionary" war,
Was no exception, to this common law

Of Great Reforms. We were unjustly taxed:
And gath'ring 'round, such men as Washington,
And John and Samuel Adams, Franklin, Floyd;
A Patrick Henry, and a Jefferson;
We spurned the thralldom of the British Crown:
For, advocating this ONE Principle,
" No taxes, without Representatives,"
We flung aside the yoke that weighed us down:
Declared ourselves; "free, independent States,"
And bought our freedom, at the price of blood.

But coming down to still more recent times:
Behold, that grand achievement of the age;
The total "Abolition" of our Curse
Of Slavery: that horrid and inhuman sin,
By which man bought and sold immortal man,
Made in the image of the Triune God;
As coolly as his cattle or his corn.
That awful traffic, had for centuries,
Been bringing curses down upon our Land,
Until its cup was full. Ah! well we know
How slowly grew that holy sentiment;
" This Nation can't continue as it is,
Half-Slave; half-free; hence Slavery must go."
At first, a very few, with voice and pen,
Dared plead the poor slave's cause; and those who did
Were called (as we are now) all sorts of names:
" Fanatics." "Fools." "Black Abolitionists."
And often at the risk of life itself,
Those true brave men, would advocate the Cause
Of Freedom, and denounce the Nation's Curse
Against fierce opposition, everywhere.

But "Abolition" was the Truth of God,
And grew, at first quite slowly, *still it grew*,
And daily, new adherents swelled its ranks.
And First, the League of Liberty" was formed;
Then came "Free-Soilers" with their ringing cry;

" Free soil, free speech, free labor and free men."
From these there sprang, in eighteen-fifty-six,
That sturdy Party, which from "Sixty-one"
To "Eighty-five," our Nation's sceptre swayed.
It was this Party's mission, under God,
To strike the shackles from the trembling slave,
And sweep this stigma from our Nation's name.
To those who say: we Prohibitionists
Have only "ONE MAIN PLANK" we answer back;
Go, read the "Platform" made in "Fifty-six:"
It had but "one main plank" From first to last,
Its theme was "Slavery" its Curse; its Cure.
And standing firmly, on that "one main plank"
It won its victory, for God and Truth.
Then let the Prohibition Party learn,
To stand on its ONE Prohibition plank,
For God Himself, is standing with us here:
At length, on this one plank, we'll win the day,
And crush the Demon Drink beneath our feet.

Our Nation's great: Our land is long and wide;
Our people more than fifty-million strong:
Hence scattered as we are; from Lakes to Gulf;
From California's coast, to distant Maine;
It takes much agitation, and much time,
Much prayer and patience, earnestness and faith;
Before some great and all-absorbing Truth,
Can sink down in, and leaven all this mass
Of human beings, so diverse in thought,
And bring them round, to view this Truth alike,
And from all stand points, see it "eye to eye."
Huge bodies must move slowly, at the first,
But once in rapid motion, they become
Almost resistless. So with some grand Truth,
Which forms the basis of a great Reform
At first it must move slowly; but ere long,
It springs from heart to heart, from lip to lip,

And bursting forth, at length, it sweeps away,
The quaking King of Error, from his throne.

Then Brother Prohibitionist! fear not.
God in His own good time and way, will show
Us His salvation, from the foe we fight.
Quite slow, thus far, has been the progress made
In slaying rum.   But let us not forget,
That in a Country, vast as is our own,
BUT ONE great Truth can be absorbed, at once,
And made the central thought, of all men's minds:
Which must be done; before a true Reform
Can be effected in a Nation's life,
Where fifty million people are concerned.
This was made clear in Eighteen Fifty-two.
The Freedom and the Temperance Reforms
Marched forward side by side.   Some thirteen States
Had passed by Statute, Prohibition laws.
But both great questions could not come at once;
Hence Prohibition was pushed back till now.
'Tis true, we have moved slowly, in the past;
But God and Truth are with us, and each day,
We gather strength, as God's omnipotence
Accelerates, our fast increasing speed,
And makes us, even now, invincible.
" In patience, let us then possess our souls,"
And learn to pray and vote, to work and wait.
It won't be long.   The bitter cup of Rum
Is almost full.   Drink's doom is nearly sealed.
Eternity's great Clock, will soon strike ONE.
Then this accursed Liquor Traffic dies,
To rise no more, till Post-Millennial days.

XIII.

In free Republics, where the People rule,
There must, from sheer necessity, exist,
At least so long as sin remains in man.

An almost constant strife, in Politics.
From these contentions, diverse "Parties" rise,
Each seeking to out-vote, and rule the rest.
'Twas always so at Rome; in Greece; and here
In our Republic, it is just the same.

The History, of these United States,
Is but the History of "Party" strife,
In constant conflict to retain or gain
Complete control of National affairs:
At times successful; oftentimes in vain;
According as the People may accept
A Party's teachings, or reject its claims.
A river does not rise above its source.
A Party, never takes a higher stand,
For Justice, Truth and Right, than that—the mass
Of those who vote its ticket, may demand.
A Party's make up, may be well compared,
To some great river deep and broad; which is
Composed of lesser rivers; these of streams.
And these again of rivulets and rills;
And these in turn are fed, by countless springs.
Our Nation's Officers; Executive;
Judicial; Legislative; represent
The mighty river: States; the larger streams;
The Counties; represent the rivulets;
The Townships; rills: Each voter is a spring.
Are springs which feed a river fresh and pure?
The waters of that river will be clear:
But if the most of them, spout mud and filth,
That river's flood will always taint the sea.
Likewise pure voters make their Party pure.
But if a large majority of those
Composing any Party are corrupt,
You strive to make that Party pure, in vain.
No Party does more than its pledge requires;
Or shouts more loudly, than its Platform speaks.

A river's mouth, proclaims its source's state;
And if the Government at Washington,
Becomes corrupt, it proves, at least this much;
That all our Nation's springs, are not yet pure.

A Party rises, pledged to some Reform:
Effects it: then becomes corrupt; and dies.
And one great Party, rights but one great wrong:
And that—the wrong she *pledged* herself, to right.
A Party rises, small at first; but true
To some grand Cause. Comes into power pure,
And for a time continues pure; because
She battles more for principles, than spoils:
Her policy is just; her motives pure;
Her Leaders also, as a rule, are true,
Brave men, whom God has fitted for their fight,
And called to bear the standard of His Truth.
A little while, these true men hold the helm,
And through God's guidance, gain the end desired.
But time works changes. Soon base men turn round,
And for the sake of popularity
And spoils, espouse the Cause they once opposed,
And quickly join the Party, which controls
The Offices they seek. Thus creeping in,
Ere long, they push aside, those pure brave men—
Who fought the battle, and secured the prize—
And seizing everywhere, with greedy hands
The reins of State and National affairs,
That once pure Party, soon becomes corrupt;
It's days are numbered, and its doom is sealed.

That Party, which arose and freed the slaves,
At first was pure; and stood before the World,
For some ten years, almost without a blot.
How has her glory waned these last few years!
Behold, her shameful, shameless "Star-Route" frauds!
Her silly "trial" of the vile Giteau!

Her base "Monopolies" and "Whiskey-Rings:"
Her vain and cowardly attempts, to please
The "Rummies" and yet hold the Temp'rance men.
" How have the Mighty fallen!"   We predict;
This once-grand-Party's course is almost run.
Those brave, true, honest, noble, Christian men,
Who constituted her great worth and strength,
Are leaving her.   And those base, selfish men,
Who by their brazen greed, have gained control,
Are wrecking her upon the rocks of wrong.
God's time has come.   Henceforth, we say; "Farewell.
We honor Thee for what Thou didst.   We go
To seek a Party, that shall do our will;
A Party pledged to smite our greatest foe,
And free us from the sting of deadly Drink."

No Party has continued to control
Our Country, more than four and twenty years
Uninterruptedly: except, when once
The Democratic Party, held the reins,
From Eighteen-One, to Eighteen-Forty-One.
The Party just dethroned, could only reach
Her four and twenty years.   And why was this?
IT WAS BECAUSE SHE WAS NOT TRUE TO GOD.
She spurned the pleadings of ten thousand tongues,
Which did not even once attempt to ask
For Prohibition; but asked simply this;
"Please grant this one small favor, and submit
This question, to the People for their votes."
According to the proverb: "Whom the gods
Are seeking to destroy, they first make mad:"
The poor Republicans, assuredly,
Were made most mad: for they rejected God,
(And Temperance, and almost all, that's right,
And pure and good; and sought the Whisky vote:
They shouted loud, "Protection for the sheep"
But dared not breath a syllable about

Protection for our precious boys and girls.
These are the reasons for their late defeat.

While on the other hand the Democrats,
In our late Election, did their best,
Worked night and day, and sought by every means,
And *any means*, to gain the Liquor vote:
For this they labored through the whole campaign;
Their leading men, their leading Journals too,
With one accord, made no attempt to hide,
Their hatred for Prohibitory laws,
Which sadly "vex our (drinking) citizens:"
They thus, have largely gained the Whisky vote,
And have succeeded. While Republicans
Attempting to retain this same vile vote,
Have lost their greatest element of strength:
For all their Temp'rance men, ere long, will join,
The Prohibition Party's swelling ranks.

The Liquor cause, has triumphed for a time;
And whisky Democrats, now rule our land.
But "night is darkest just before the dawn"
So, Herod-like, while making loudest boasts,
And seemingly, the Conqueror of all,
Drink shall be stricken, and go down to death.
For God shall smite this Demon, "Not by might
Nor Pow'r, but by His Spirit" and the rule
Of Rum, in this free land, will not last long:
For roused to action, by the silent force,
Of this Eternal Spirit's matchless might,
Our fifty million freemen, will not long
Allow themselves, like slaves, to lie beneath,
The feet, of half a million Liquor Lords;
Nor suffer them to squander every year,
Two billion dollars worth of hard earned wealth,
And sink one-hundred thousand souls to Hell,
And fill, at least, five million homes with woe.

How long shall these vile, wicked men, who sit
Unmoved, by childrens' cries, or woman's tears,
Control with beer-bought votes, our Government?
They rule us now; but THEY CAN'T RULE US LONG.
Our Cause is growing stronger each campaign,
And Prohibition votes will multiply,
Until at last, perhaps by Eighty-Eight, (?)
Or if not then, at least by Ninety-two,
A Prohibition flag will wave above
Our Country's Capitol; and in that House,
Where Garfield suffered, and where Lincoln died,
We'll place a Prohibition President,
Some fearless man, who will be proud to plead
The Cause of God, against the curse of Rum.
Is this, think you, a visionary dream?
Just bide the march of history, and see,
How God—before the setting Sun shall sink
Behind the Nineteenth Century—shall cause
This humble prophecy, to be fulfilled.
" *Oh Lord, not our will, but Thine be done!*"

XIV.

'Tis constantly affirmed, "We do not need
Another Party, to take up this work:
Let no new Party have a moment's thought,
But only let the old ones be reformed."

Some things, like Satan, cannot be reformed."
These Parties are corrupt, and are controlled
Almost exclusively, by wicked men,
Who care for nothing, but to seize the spoils;
And to this end they bend their Party's vote,
And laugh to think, how good true men are duped.
They say, "Begin down low, and then go up;
Go to the 'Primaries' and let good men,

Elect none but good men, until they fill
Each 'Office,' from 'Trustee' to 'President:'
Then all the Framers of our Country's laws,
And all her Officers will be good men.''
In theory, perhaps this plan might do;
But when it comes to practice, IT WON'T WORK.
It does not reckon on the Devil's might;
Nor count the numbers of his hostile hosts;
Nor measure up the wealth and strength of sin;
Nor know the malice of resisted wrong.
Just for example, let good Temp'rance men
Attend the "Primaries" of these two good (?)
Old Parties, and attempt to advocate,
The putting of a Prohibition plank
Into the Party Platform.   As a rule,
Such acts, would rouse at once, most bitter strife,
And if persisted in, would quickly rend
Their Party into fragments; for like oil
And water, Truth and Error will not mix,
Nor Prohibition ever blend with Rum.

One stubborn fact, is often overlooked;
OLD PARTIES NEVER TAKE UP NEW REFORMS,
WHEN THESE REFORMS INVOLVE MAJORITIES.
That is; in politics, no Party will
Espouse a Cause, which when it is espoused,
The Party Leaders know, 'twill drive away
Enough of votes, to swell the other side,
And bring upon their own side sure defeat.
'Tis for this reason, all with one accord,
Republicans and Democrats alike,
Refuse to take up Prohibition's Cause;
Although the best men in both Parties know,
It is the Cause of God and Truth and Right.
The Party Leaders, in both Parties, see:
If Prohibition is espoused; at once
They lose the Liquor vote, for Liquor men,

Are not Republicans nor Democrats,
But "WHISKYITES;" and do not hesitate,
To leave, their "dear old Party" should it lean
The least bit, toward the Prohibition side.
And thus, since PROHIBITION DOES INVOLVE
" MAJORITIES;" both Parties are alike
Afraid to touch it. *Both still cling to Rum.*
Republicans well know, that if they lose,
The Democrats will gain their whisky vote:
Also upon the other hand, **they** know
That if they should espouse the cause of **Rum,**
Their Temp'rance vote will go, and that no less
Means sure defeat. Hence in perplexity,
We see, this "great progressive (?) Party" stand
And try to look and talk two ways at once.
Such milk and water policy deserved,
And justly terminated in defeat.
" A house divided, cannot stand." No more
Can any Party, rent by factious strife.
Republicans, in North Carolina say:
" We want free rum. No Prohibition here;"
But listen to them up in grand old Maine;
In Iowa or Kansas, hear them shout:
" No longer will we bear the curse of Drink,
Hurrah for Prohibition from this foe!"
Thus in its vain attempts, to do two things,
And advocate two principles at once
Directly opposite; this Party has
Been digging for itself a speedy grave;
And when it dies, its tomb will taste few tears;
For on the "head-stone," all will see inscribed:
" DIED ON THE BATTLE-FIELD OF DRINK, BETWEEN
THE HOSTS OF PROHIBITION, AND OF RUM."

How foolish, for Republicans to say:
" You blind, Third Party, Prohibitionists
Defeated us: and we will never have

Another thing to do with Temp'rance work."
Please don't "bite off your nose, to spite your face."
Such foolish and revengeful talk may do,
For those vile Politicians, who desire
To see their Party win; although it costs
Them everything that's just and right and good;
But *never* will it do for Christian men.
As well assert: "We'll do no more for God,
Unless He works, according to our plans."
Republicans! You cannot help yourselves.
You *must* take up this blessed cause of God.
You are defeated, and can never rise;
Until you leave your beer-bought Party's ranks,
And come and join God's Prohibition hosts.
Some good men say, and many of them think,
The late Republican defeat, has set
The cause of Temp'rance back for many years.
Poor timid ones! "O ye of little faith."
" Shall not the Judge of all the Earth do right?"
How can it set the cause of Temp'rance back?
Can things be any worse than they are now?

What claim have you Republicans, upon
The Temp'rance people of this wine-cursed Land?
If you had still continued to control
Our Government, how soon, we humbly ask,
Would you have freed us, from the curse of Drink?
When you first took the reins of Government,
There were some thirteen States, which had declared'
For Prohibition, making it their law.
Where are those Prohibition laws to-day?
Repealed. Except in Iowa and Maine.
Repealed by whom? By you Republicans.
Perhaps you point to Kansas, and exclaim;
" See how we carried Prohibition there."
If thousands of good Temp'rance Democrats,
Had not joined in, and helped you with their votes,

You would have failed ingloriously. Why not
Give *them* some credit, for the victory?
But granting, you, Republicans have freed,
A solitary State, from Drink's dire curse:
Still this most awful, stubborn fact, remains;
That while Republicans have ruled our land,
The Drunkard-making business, has increased,
Compared with our Population's growth,
At least THREE TIMES AS FAST. We ask once more,
Can such a Party's overthrow, set back
The Temp'rance Cause, so many years? Ah, No!
For blessed be our God! No Party can,
By its defeat, o'erthrow God's holy Cause.
Both men and Parties, may go down to death,
But Truth triumphant, treads eternal years.

Some say, "We Prohibitionists, denounce
Republicans, far more than Democrats."
The truth is we denounce them both alike.
A large majority of Temp'rance men,
Throughout the Northern and the Western States,
Have been, and are to-day, Republicans:
And owing to their fear of Southern rule,
Have idolized their Party, and refused
To see its glaring faults. Hence God arose,
And smote their Idol. Set its captives free.
The South now rules; and yet "The Government
At Washington still lives." Republicans,
Who are not still blind partisans, now see,
Or will see soon. That they were sold to Rum,
And that all Temp'rance men, must now combine,
And as one man, attack the Democrats.

Ye Temp'rance Democrats! Come forth! Come forth!
Oh! join us in this battle, for the Truth!
This fight, "For God and Home and Native Land!"
Your Democratic Party, where is it?

Sold! SOLD!! Completely sold, to deep-dyed Drink.
Without a blush, it courts the smiles of Rum,
And under covert of its constant cry,
·' No SUMPTUARY LAWS" it bows the knee
To King Gambrinus, and implores his aid,
To lift it into power. Oh! How long
Will Christian men continue to support
A party founded on the curse of Rum,
And boldly boasting of its league with Hell?
From neither Party, can we hope for help,
To stem the tide of drunkenness and woe:
Some great new Party must and will be formed;
Which coming up, will stand a changeless rock,
Against which, BOTH OLD PARTIES shall be wrecked.

The need of this is seen, when we reflect;
How members of the two old Parties hate,
And villify each other. Now suppose,
Republicans should advocate the Cause
Of Prohibition. Would those Democrats
Who are, and always have been Temp'rance men,
Become Republicans, and straightway join
The Party, they have hated all their lives?
Experience and reason answer, No!
Or, if it could be possible (?) suppose,
The Democratic Party, should espouse
The Cause of Prohibition, do you think
All good, true, Temperance Republicans,
Would rush into the Democratic ranks?
Would they not say; "This is another dodge,
To seize upon the Governmental reins?"
But as our grand, new Temp'rance Party now
Advances to the front; it will not need,
To overcome this old time hate, mistrust,
And Party prejudice; but holding forth,
God's just, eternal, holy blessed Truth
Of Prohibition, it will soon unite,

And link together both in North and South,
All Temp'rance men and women, old and young,
Of every Party, and of every class:
And in due time, when all the good, are found,
In one grand Party, it will not be long,
Till God shall crown that Party with success.
God speed the day, when both Republican,
And Democratic leadership, shall end,
And "Prohibitionists" shall rule our Land!

They say: "We are not READY yet for this."
When shall we then be ready, if we fail
To go to work at once, and get ourselves,
And those around us, ready for the fray?
One thing is certain, we shall *never* be
Prepared for Prohibition, just so long
As we give heed to that old well-known wail,
Wrung from the vile Rum-selling Ring: "Don't! *Don't!!*
Oh Don't!!! Take Temp'rance into Politics"!!!
May all true Christian men soon see the Right,
And seeing, VOTE, AS GOD SHALL GIVE THEM LIGHT.

Despite the sneers and lies, of liquor lords,
The principle of Prohibition, rests
Upon the basis of Eternal Truth;
And stands, and will forever stand, as firm;
Amid all Liquor-Dealers' fierce assaults;
As does the Rock whose changeless base is fixed
In Earth's deep bosom, out mid Ocean's depths;
Unmoved, it laughs, to hear the Ocean moan,
And bids defiance, to its fiercest waves,
Which seek, in vain, to shake its rock-bound base.
Thus Prohibition laughs at raging Rum,
And bids defiance to its fierce attacks;
For well she knows, her own God-given strength,
Can always, stem the fury of her foes.

XV.

These chief objections, urged against our Cause,
Have been thus answered, fairly we believe:
Now let us turn, and view a few strong points,
Which singly, and combined, most clearly prove,
That Prohibition is the cause of God,
And, for humanity, a priceless boon.

And First. IT IS NO COMPROMISE WITH SIN.
It strikes a deadly blow, not at the *bark*,
But at the very *heart* of Rum's dire curse.
All other remedies, at best, seek but
To wound; this seeks to *slay* the demon Drink.
With Drink, as with all other crimes and wrongs,
Supply creates demand, a law diverse
From that which holds in honest trades, for there
Demand creates supply, but with Drink's trade,
And every sin, the greater the supply,
The greater the demand will always be.
Now, to prohibit drink cuts off at once
The vile supply, and thus soon stops demand,
For liquor appetites are all acquired;
And if their cause can only be removed
They soon must cease.   Now nothing is more true
Than that, so long as this vile drink *is made*
IT WILL BE DRANK.   But prohibition stops
Its manufacture and its sale, alike,
(Except for medicine and useful arts),
And thus dries up the fountain of its curse,
And quenches, for all time, its stream of woe.

To render vipers harmless, no man thinks
Of burning off their tails.   He draws their fangs.
Or, better still, *takes off their hissing heads.*
Let Temp'rance workers, then, no longer strive

To scorch the tail of this dread Demon Drink
With these poor "license" torches; but at once,
Oh, let us seize our Prohibition swords,
And soon, by bold, persistent, well-aimed blows,
Smite off this deadly monster's hydra-head.
This has been done in Maine, and other States,
Where Prohibition has been fairly tried.

Throughout all Maine not one vile brewery,
Or still more vile distillery, is found.
By Prohibition, Rum is quickly slain,
And nothing less will ever lay it low.
Talk not of compromise. 'Tis worse than vain.
How true, that quaint old proverb, which runs thus:
" He who eats soup with Satan finds quite soon
He needs a wondrously long-handled spoon."
Think you that God will bless a league with hell,
Or prosper any compromise with wrong?
Look at our late red-handed war and learn
How vain it is to compromise with sin.
For years 'twas nothing else but compromise.
With all its bitter fruits of blight and blood,
We only sought to let this slave trade be,
Provided it would not encroach upon
" Free" territory. But, like Banquo's ghost,
" It would not down." The whole accursed trade
In slaves was wrong, and God had sealed its doom.
His time had come and slavery must die.
All sorts of compromises failed. At last
That party which must put it down arose.
But even it was blinded, and instead
Of taking "Freedom" for its corner-stone,
It compromised the truth of God, and said,
" We must put down rebellion in the States,
But if this slave-trade stays where it is now,
Then we will be content." But God said, "No!
This whole vile trade must go." Then came the war,

And brothers' hands were bathed in brothers' blood.
For almost two long, bloody years they fought,
Yet Freedom's cause had not advanced.   Defeat,
In quick succession, followed up defeat.
And why? GOD WAS AN "ABOLITIONIST,"
And nothing else would satisfy Him, save
An "unconditional surrender" to
His righteous terms.   *"The whole slave trade must go."*
He could not bless a compromise with wrong,
And hence, up to the close of "Sixty Two,"
The armies of the North had scarcely won
A signal victory, and all looked dark.
At last our martyred Lincoln sees God's terms,
" We must accept these terms.   We have been wrong.
These dark-skinned millions must go free at once,
If we would win this conflict for the right,
And save our country from the curse of God."

On New Year's morning, Eighteen-sixty-three,
Our President declared "all captives free,"
And from that blessed day "No compromise
With Slavery " became our country's cry.
And now God smiles upon his battling hosts,
For, from that happy day, they scarcely lost
A single battle, worthy of the name.
They had "closed in with God," and all is light,
And joy, and peace.   The flag of freedom floats
O'er all, and "Abolition" reigns supreme.

From this disastrous compromise with sin
Let Prohibitionists a lesson learn.
Let us AT FIRST, accept God's righteous terms,
And shun all compromise from friend or foe,
For only thus can we expect to win
In this fierce conflict with the Fiend of rum.
It is not true, as some pretend to say,
" That had the abolitionists refused

To enter into any compromise
With slavery, they never could have gained
The victory they finally achieved."
No man can ever make another man
A better one by doing wrong with him.
If we would greatly bless and help our race,
And lift men out of sorrow, sin, and shame,
We must, ourselves, stand on a higher plane;
And then, instead of going down to them
To share their sin. They must come up to us.
Should we thus stoop to them, all would be lost,
For, in their just contempt, they then would cry,
" Physician heal thyself." No, nevermore,
Did man, at any time, win any man
From any sin, by partnership therein.

GOD EVER BLESSES THOSE WHO DO THE RIGHT.
And had the abolitionists stood firm
And boldly shunned all compromising schemes
God would have blessed their battles *from the first,*
And then, instead of four long years of blood,
Far sooner had Truth triumphed. And who knows (?)
Perhaps without our dreadful war at all.

As all things, short of abolition, failed
To free us from the curse of slavery,
So nothing short of "Constitutional"
And universal Prohibition will
Forever free us from the curse of Drink;
And all because IT IS NO COMPROMISE.
For this alone, and nothing less than this,
Can claim the blessing of that holy God,
Who in His decalogue lays down this law,
That Prohibition, simple, plain, and pure,
Without the shadow of a compromise,
Is always Heaven's only cure for crime.

XVI.

And Second.   Prohibition WILL REDUCE
OUR TAXES.   *Nothing taxes us like Rum.*
Some people—many people think, because
Our revenues from Drink are very large,
That this great Liquor Traffic pays its way,
Or more than pays its way; and on account
Of these vast revenues it really is
A great advantage to the Government
And to the People.   *What a dread mistake !!!*
There's nothing cheats us like this liquor trade,
Or burdens us so heavily as Drink.
Whence do our heavy taxes come?   From schools
And colleges?   Or from our churches?   No!
They always largely flow from Alcohol.

When we remember that at least four-fifths
Of all the criminals within our jails
And penitentiaries throughout our land,
And that two-thirds of all our pauper hosts,
And that one-half of those who are insane,
And that a large per cent. of blind and dumb,
And idiotic children, everywhere,
Who must be cared for by the Government,
Are all but bitter clusters from one vine,
The poisoned vine of Drink;   And when we know
That all that mighty army now engaged
In this infernal traffic must be fed,
And kept, and clothed, by hard earned wages wrung,
From streaming brows, and sun-burnt blistered hands,
Which in our work-shops, and upon our soil,
Are constantly at work to pay these bills,
Thus laid upon us, by our liquor tax:
Rememb'ring these sad facts, is there no call
For Prohibition?   For statistics show,

And righteousness and reason teach the same,
That Prohibition, soon will sweep away
These heavy whisky taxes. Nevermore,
Until this curse is banished from our Land;
Will we begin to fully realize
How sorely we were taxed for its support.

XVII.

While Prohibition makes our taxes light;
It does still more. It strikes a fatal blow,
Against Unjust Monopolies, and thus
Must greatly benefit all " lab'ring men."
For Prohibition utterly destroys
The largest, and beyond all doubt, the *worst*
Monopoly, that ever cursed our Earth.

The constant conflict, going on to-day,
Between our working-men and millionaires;
Our Capital and Labor; Wealth and Work;
Is one of vast importance to the world;
One, on the settlement of which, depend
The weal or woe, of multitudes of men.
In this great struggle, vast monopolies,
Must ever hold a place of prominence.
Now great Monopolies are not all bad,
And in their proper place and sphere, may do,
(As many do) a vast amount of good.
But some, are wholly, always, only bad;
And such is this Monopoly of Rum.
Not one redeeming feature can it boast.

In this broad land of ours, bound with bands
Of steel, both North and South, and East and West;
The very moment, mention may be made
Of great Monopolies; at once, men think

Of Railroads, as the greatest of them all:
Not so, for millions upon millions more,
Of hard-earned wealth are wasted, aye, far worse
Than wasted, on this heartless, beastly, vile
Monopoly of Liquor; than are spent
For Railroads, or on any other trade
Or traffic under Heaven. Go if you can,
And estimate the good already done,
By our great Railway systems; though no doubt,
They have committed many direful wrongs,
In trampling under foot God's Holy day,
And "grinding down the faces of the poor,"
Still, on the whole, with all their faults, they help
And bless our Land.   But what has whisky done?

Oh, Fellow-Countrymen ! Do we now groan,
Beneath the heavy hands of want and wrong?
Behold ! that vast Monopoly of Sin,
Which lifts its head so high above all else,
And flings its lurid flames across the World !
It is the Devil's traffic in Strong Drink:
Our greatest foe: Rum's vile monopoly:
And worst of all, OUR GOVERNMENT CREATES
This vast, unjust monopoly, BY LAW:
The State steps in and says, "A chosen few,"
(*Those base enough to do this fiendish work,*)
" Shall share the profits of this Godless trade."

But who supports this vile monopoly ?
Who feeds its fires and furnishes its funds?
THE WORKING-MAN. *At least fifteen per cent.*
Of all the earnings of our Working-men,
Goes in to line the pockets, of those poor,
Deluded, greatly-to-be-pitied Fools,
Those soul-destroying, liquor-dealing Knaves,
Who for some paltry gold, will sell their all.

Far better, would it be for Working-men,
If they, instead of going to our Millionaires,
And there demanding from them, "bread or blood"
Should march in solid phalanx to the polls,
And with their ballots, *slay the Demon Drink:*
For he, by all odds, is their greatest foe;
And his, is the Monopoly of all
Monopolies, which *always* stands opposed
To every int'rest of the Working-man.

The Liquor-dealers always try to make,
The Working-classes think, they are their friends:
Just as the spider is the fly's best friend,
Until he gets him safely in his web ;—
Just so, these Liquor-Sellers pat the backs,
Of Working-men, so long as they can sell,
Death-dealing Drink to them, for hard-earned gold:
But mark you,—when they drain their last poor cent
From them,—they cooly kick them out of doors.

Come. Fellow-Workmen, from your dusty fields,
Or still more dusty shops, and let us smite,
This mighty, moneyed monster of Strong Drink:
With Prohibition, we can soon destroy,
This one, vast, vile monopoly of Rum,
And clothe with comfort, every child of toil,
And crown our humble Homes with lasting Peace.

XVIII.

And Fourthly. Prohibition, WILL PROMOTE
FREE EDUCATION, in our Land; and all
Right-minded men, admit that this is one
Main stone, upon which rests, our Nation's hope.
And all wise-thinkers, feel that every hand,
Which strikes a fatal blow, against our schools,

Seals up the Fountain of our liberties,
And flings us back, into that night, from which
The World emerged, four hundred years ago.

Against all colleges and schools, to-day,
A cruel hand is raised to strike a blow,
Which though it may not kill, still sadly wounds.
Our precious colleges, and public schools,
And which, unless removed, may some day crush,
The Cause of Education, ever dear,
To all who love the Truth, and seek the Light.
This hand so hostile to our Country's schools,
Is hidden now; but soon will be unearthed:
Then all, as some do now, will clearly see;
It is the cruel hand of blind-eyed Rum,
Which seeks to bind us, with its iron chains,
And snuff the candle of our knowledge out.

We ask: whose children, schooled in every vice,
Grow up in ignorance? Whose children have
No books, nor clothes, nor yet encouragement
To go to school? Almost in every case,
They are the children of those drunken ones,
Who sink their earnings, in the bowl of death.
Three-fourths of those who are illiterate,
In this, the Land of almost countless schools,
Are those, whose fathers, or whose mothers use
Intoxicating drinks; and thus are made,
Incompetent, as well as disinclined,
To send their children, to our grand free schools.

Now in this Country, where there is no law,
(Yet where undoubtedly, there should be one,)
Compelling children to attend our schools;
And in this Country, where there are to-day,
Permitted and sustained, by statute law,
At least two-hundred thousand liquor dens,

Where ignorance and vice, are freely taught,
In open opposition to our schools,—
In such a land, can any think it strange;
That, by the hundred thousands, boys and girls
Are growing up, who never go to school?

The greatest dangers, to our Government,
And to our Institutions free, are those
Which always spring from ignorance and vice,
And these, we know, spring largely from Strong Drink.
Yet all this time, our Government upholds,
A licensed Groggery, on every hand,
Where by the million, wretched children may,
Receive an education, most complete,
In all the rudiments of sin and shame,
As well as in the higher grades of vice,
And crime; and whence, ere long, they will obtain,
Diplomas of full graduation, from
These Universities of wholesale Hell,—
On which Diplomas, are these pregnant words,
These sad, heart-rending words, "Drink!   *Drunkard!*
    DEATH!"

Oh, will not God's grand, holy, blessed Cause,
Of full, free Education, be advanced,
When these low, liquor-licensed schools of vice,
These colleges of cruelty and crime,
These Universities of endless Death,
Shall all be swept forever from our Earth,
By just and righteous Prohibition laws?

And let one word be spoken here, we pray,
For those poor slaves who were at last set free,
But whose dark minds, untaught for ages past,
When, in a moment, brought into the light
Of Freedom's blazing, burning, noonday sun,
Were dazed, and could not bear its brilliant beams,

But sank back into ignorance and gloom.
They thus became a prey for every form
Of vice, oppression, violence and fraud.

This is not true, by any means, of ALL;
For many of our brightest, keenest minds,
Once bent beneath the burdens of the slave:
These, since their Freedom's dawn, have so improved,
That, bursting through the bonds which bound their
    hands,
And those still stronger bonds of ignorance
Which bound their minds, they stand to-day, the peers
Of any race, in any age or clime.

Though this be true of some, yet this sad fact
Remains. That millions of our " Freedman's " race
Can neither read nor write, and lying low
In ignorance, they readily become
The dupes of those vile knaves, who know the right
And yet who always choose to do the wrong,
And who, like very fiends, make other mens'
Misfortunes stepping stones to lift themselves
Up into lives of luxury and ease.

Oh, shall we not defend this helpless race,
To which, for years of unpaid toil, we owe
A debt of most enormous magnitude?
Oh, shall we not attempt to help them break
These bonds of ignorance which bind them fast,
That they may soon behold Truth's wondrous light
And spurn their present bondage to those knaves
Who, through their ignorance, still make them slaves?

There is but one true way to grant them help.
'Tis this. THEY MUST BE TAUGHT TO HELP THEMSELVES.
To feel the need of colleges and schools.
Now NEVER will this object be attained

Until the manufacture and the sale
Of all intoxicating drinks is stopped.
For all admit, THE FREEDMAN'S CURSE IS RUM.
And thousands of these poor benighted souls,
Who once bemoaned the slavery of men,
Are now, with chains ten thousand times as strong,
Bound down forever, by the demon Drink,
Beneath the awful SLAVERY OF HELL.

Oh, shall we, as a Nation, be aroused
From North to South, from East to West, and sink
Four billion dollars and one million men
To sweep away the slavery of man,
Then, sitting down with folded hands, refuse
To even lift a finger to destroy
The curse of rum, the slavery of Hell?
Oh, let us heed the cries of former slaves,
And save them from a still more fearful fate,
By banishing forever from our land
This traffic in Strong Drink! And then in place
Of "gin-mills" we'll have churches, and instead
Of vile saloons, **"the breathing holes of Hell,"**
Where ignorance and vice go hand in hand,
We'll have grand colleges and common schools,
And then the FREEDMAN'S PROBLEM WILL BE SOLVED.

Hurrah, for Prohibition! 'Tis the friend
Of EDUCATION and of all that's good,
And comes to liberate the slaves of Drink,
And shed God's light on Rum-benighted minds.

XIX.

Another thing will Prohibition do.
'TWILL LARGELY HELP TO BLESS AND PURIFY
THE GREAT AND GROWING CITIES, of our land.
These cities are the centers of our life:

We look to their great busy marts for trade;
Into their laps we pour our choicest gifts;
Within their bosom rests our greatest wealth;
Twelve millions of our people press their streets,
And many millions more are crowding fast
Into their homes (already more than full)
In ever rapidly increasing throngs.
In eighteen-hundred, but *one twenty-fifth*
Of all the people had their homes, 'tis said,
In our great cities.   Now, at least *one-fifth*
Of all our population (though increased
So vastly) may be found within the bounds
Of these great centers of our nation's life

Now, if the vast majority of those
Who thus have filled our cities were good men,
The very best of all our people, then
This tendency to centralize our power
By massing most of these, our growing hosts,
Into a few great cities, would not be
The cause of any danger to the State.
But such, alas, has never been the case!
For while 'tis true that many of our best
And noblest men and women have their homes
In these large cities, yet 'tis just as true
(However sad the fact) that wicked men
Out-number, in the cities all the good.
The weak and vain, the idle, and the vile,
Attracted by the glare of city life,
Or by its greater opportunities
For exercising every gift of brain,
To get a living without honest toil,
Or for committing every kind of crime,
Have flocked into our cities, more and more,
Until they hold almost complete control
Of nearly every city in the land.
Controlled by vile Monoplies and Rings,

Our cities have become our greatest shame.
They are the haunts of vice and crime and lust.
Some portions of them have become so vile,
That if one dared to designate their name
They would be rightly called,—**"Hot-beds of Hell"**
Where Devils plan and act through human fiends.

There is one curse, which towers high above
All others in our cities, and which works
More ruin, and creates more want and woe,
Produces more real wretchedness and wrong,
Than all the rest combined. It is the curse,
The awful, universal curse of Rum,
Which turns our cities into haunts of vice,
And makes them synonyms for shames and crimes;
The vile abodes of everything unjust and mean;
Of all impurity and beggary and sin.

A problem more momentous, than the one
Which centers in "Municipal control"
Can scarcely be conceived; For 'tis a fact
Large Cities rule the World, and these in turn
Are largely ruled by base and wicked men.
Hence, very frequently you hear it said;
And often even Temp'rance men believe,
" That Prohibition will succeed in towns,
And in our rural regions, well enough.
But in great Cities, it will prove a farce."

Well let us bravely look *facts*, in the face.
It is a fact, that not a single State
Has carried Prohibition, in whose bounds
Is any City of important size.
It also is a fact, that in the five
Chief Cities of Ohio, we have found,
Our Prohibition vote was "counted out."
It is a fact, that nearly all our "Strikes"

And "Riots," in our Cities, have their birth.
It is a fact. Municipal misrule
Is our chief danger; and that hellish Rum
Its chief support, holds Cities in His hand.
It is a fact: That "Primaries" of both
Old Parties meet, quite often in Saloons.
It is a fact. That in our City Courts
Corruption is the rule, till Justice mocked;
Our streets have frequently run red with blood.
It is a most appalling fact, That vice
And "Anarchy" and all high-handed crimes,
That violence and strife; that discontent
And hatred, by the poor, against the rich;
Are in our Cities daily growing worse;
Till "Politics" in both old Parties, is
A most disgraceful scramble for "the spoils;"
A game of "buy and sell" by "Party hacks"
And "Boodle Bosses" who well understand,
" Whoever wins, the Victors, **'must divide.'** "

With all these dreadful facts before our eyes,
Shall we give up our battle for the Right ?
Must " Universal Suffrage " be repealed ?
Shall wicked Liquor men, our Cities rule,
And ruling, ruin all we hold most dear ?
Shall " Anarchists " and howling mobs demand,
Unless we all bow down to their sweet will
They'll wreck our cities and burn up our homes,
Or send their bullets crashing through our brain ?

The craven coward, in a time like this,
Would basely cry, " yes! yes! we will submit!"
Not so, those patriots, in whose blue viens
Is flowing hot the blood of dauntless sires.
No! no! we'll die first!" is their fearless shout.
We prophesy that George C. Haddock's blood
Is not the last the demon Drink shall spill.

" There's no remission where no blood is shed."
This seems to be the law of all reforms.
Hence, though not pessimistic, we feel sure
That rum will never die a peaceful death.
The fiercest of the fight will never come
Until the prohibitionists succeed
In national elections.   Not till then
Will come " the tug of war." for we will find
Electing prohibition easy work
Compared with its ENFORCEMENT.   Our late war
Came *after* Lincoln's triumph, NOT BEFORE.

Hence, after prohibitionists elect
Their President and Congress, they will find
Their hardest battle will be to enforce
Prohibitory laws within the bounds
Of all our largest cities.   And although
The prohibition party will not cause
Another civil war, yet we predict
Most fierce and bloody riots in our streets;
For whisky men (law-breakers that they are),
Defying openly that wise restraint
Forbidding any man to sell Strong Drink,
Upon election days; they'll deal it out
Like water, to their poor deluded dupes,
Until with maddened brain, led on by knaves
And liquor cut-throats, those half-drunken mobs
Will shout, " DOWN WITH THESE PROHIBITION CRANKS
WHO WANT TO TAKE AWAY OUR LIBERTIES."
Unchecked by "Officers" in league with them
They'll rush around the " ballot box " with guns,
Revolvers, sticks, and stones, and drive away
The prohibition voter from the " polls."
But such mob violence will not last long.
The People's will in any righteous cause
Becomes invincible.   A few brave souls
Will seal their testimony to the truth

With their life's blood.   But righteousness will win.
And let this be remembered.   That no State
Cursed with large cities will be competent
To cope unaided with these " whisky mobs."
The arm to wield the hammer which shall break
Drink's deadly curse to pieces will not be
The puny arm of any single State;
'Twill be the Nation's, in that Party's hands,
Which God is raising up, to sweep Strong Drink
From every town and city in the land.

Once give us Prohibition, and we know,
The problem of our cities will be solved:
That very soon they all will be transformed,
From reeking hot-beds of all kinds of crime,
Of cruelty and poverty and woe;
Into the peaceful joyous blest abodes,
Of healthy, happy children, women, men;
A people pious, temperate and wise,
Their hearts and homes forever freed from Rum.

XX.

Moreover Prohibition will procure;
God's richest blessings to those very men,
Who now are fighting it.   Poor wretched souls !
Deluded by their greedy thirst for gold,
They can not—will not see their greatest good.
They do not seem to know, their traffic is,
Their greatest curse.   That while they cling to Rum,
They press a deadly viper to their hearts,
Which is most surely, stinging them to death—
An endless death—   And yet they know it not.
Shall none of these poor wretched ones be saved ?
Oh yes!   Thank God!   Great numbers of them shall.
God's holy Prohibition will compel,

These men, to quit this business, which destroys
Alike, the life of others, and their own,
And force them to take up some honest trade.

No business is so "hardening" as this
Of selling Drink, and none degrades so soon.
The Liquor-Dealer can not help but see
What harm he does.   He sees his victims grow
More ragged and more wretched, day by day—
He often listens to the trembling tones,
Of some pale starving boy or shiv'ring girl,
Who stand with streaming eyes, and plead with him;
" Please Mister" (Drunkard-Maker) " Please, oh, PLEASE!
Don't sell my father any more strong drink "—
He hears of some poor drunkard's noble wife,
Or good old mother, laid to rest—whose hearts
He knows full well, were broken by *his* Rum.

No wonder these poor wretches steel themselves
Against the claims of pity—otherwise
Their hearts hard as they are, *would surely break*.
But do they quit their trade ? No, no! not they !
They take another glass of hellish Drink,
And soon forget the ruin they have wrought;
But God the Righteous One does not forget;
For all these things are written in His Book,
And His deep curse rests on this whole vile trade:
Hence though 'tis true, these Liquor-Dealers make
Vast sums of money, by their horrid work,
Yet it is always at the price of health,
Or happiness.   No man can ever be,
A happy man, whose conscience feels the guilt,
Of him, whose riches are the fruits of fraud.

These Liquor-Dealers seldom live long lives.
They nearly always soon become the slaves
Of Drink, and die the drunkard's hopeless death.

They often die from violence and strife,
Or often kill themselves, through dread remorse.
There are to them, but few enjoyments *here*;
And in the Great Hereafter, ALL IS GLOOM.
They have no true peace in the present world ;
No pleasant prospects, in the World to Come.
Oh, this whole business is most ruinous!
And many Liquor-Dealers know it well:
And doubtless THOUSANDS who are now engaged
In this degraded and degrading trade,
Would gladly quit it, if they *thought* they could.

True Temperance Reformers do not hate,
These Liquor men; but each Reformer feels,
" Oh would to God ! that I could take the hand
Of every Liquor-Dealer on the Globe,
And lift him out of Drink's most sick'ning filth,
Into a life of righteousness and truth."
And by God's grace, in His own time, WE WILL.

Dear Fellow-Workers, in this grand Reform !
That happy day is not far distant now;
When many of these poor, blind, Liquor men,
Converted and reformed, will bless their God,
For these same Temp'rance men; who now are called
By them.   " Fanatics, Hypocrites and Fools."
Yes, Prohibition will most surely bring,
To every Liquor-Dealer boundless good,
And prove his richest blessing; For no doubt,
In many cases, it will set him free,
Not only from the guilt of selling Rum,
But from the rule of Satan and of Sin;
And through resistless grace, based on the blood
And righteousness of Christ; the Holy Ghost
Will lift him out of darkness into Light,
And place upon his head, " the crown of life."

XXI.

Still further, Prohibition WILL BREAK UP
THE "SOLID SOUTH" and "solid North" as well.
Philanthropists, both North and South, had hoped;
That when the war had ended strife would cease,
And that old hatred, which had cursed our Land
So many years would soon become extinct :—
That Love would soon cement divided hearts,
And bury evermore fraternal feuds,
By healing up the wounds of civil strife.
Alas ! for human hopes ! It is not so.
We find the South arrayed against the North,
Almost as bitterly, as in those days,
When Slavery so sorely tried men's souls.
Now this hostility must be removed,
Or else the Nation's life is still at stake.
Why all this bitter sectional abuse ?
Why all this hatred ? Why a " Solid South ? "
And why, opposing it, a " Solid North ? "
What is the cause for such a state of things ?
Is Slavery this cause ? It can't be that:
For in the South, they are as much opposed
To Slavery to-day, as in the North.

Here is the cause. We have a solid North,
Arrayed against a Solid South, because,
WE *will* NOT *bury* ISSUES THAT ARE *Dead.*
Both sides are very much to blame for this.
Our civil war, which sealed forevermore
The doom of Slavery, was waged long since,
And settled that great question, *for all time.*

Alas ! most all our Politicians fail,
To fully realize, this blessed fact.
They seem to be, still list'ning to the din

Of clashing arms; or down beneath the dense
Black smoke, of deadly battle, they still seem,
To see, the flowing of fraternal blood;
And hence, instead of reaching forth the hand
Of peace, across the gulf of civil strife,
And healing with the touch of tender Love,
The deep-laid wounds inflicted by the war;
They seem to take a fiendish, strange delight,
In op'ning up afresh these closing wounds;
Thus kindling up anew, the smould'ring fires
Of cruel hate.   When will such conduct melt
Our stubborn hearts, and weld us into one ?

Let any candid and unbiased man (?)
Aside from Party prejudice, review
The " Campaign " work, of Platform and of Press,
For twelve years past.   And let him take this work,
From both great Parties, treating them alike,
And let him pour the whole vast putrid mass,
Into the golden crucible of Truth;
And he will find, when he has boiled it down,
He only has a pitiful rehash,
Of old dead issues, settled long ago.

Our Politicians have for twenty years,
Been harping on the old and worn-out strings,
Of " Slavery."   " The Sovereignty of States."
" Secession," and such kindred thread-bare themes.
No wonder then, we have a solid South,
And solid North.   We always will be rent
Asunder thus; until we leave these dead,
Old issues, slumbering beneath the sod
Of brotherly forgetfulness: and take
Some new and living question up,
Connected with the common needs of each
And every Section of our common Land.

Where can we find this question, do you ask?
God, angels, men, all seem to answer back.
" What question of more vital interest—
More vast importance, to the North and South,
The East and West, than this of Temperance?"

Just think a moment. **Talk about the war!**
Why we destroy, more money and more men,
Each year, by our accursed liquor trade;
Than were destroyed, in any single year,
Of our late deadly and disastrous war.
And Gladstone, truly says. "Intemperance
Destroys more of our English-speaking race,
Than Famine, War and Pestilence combined."

Was our whole **Nation**, stirred, **awakened, wild,**
Because of Slavery? And shall we **sleep,**
With folded hands, untouched, and unaroused,
By this far viler Slavery of Rum?
Oh, *no*! NO!! NO!!! It can not—*shall* not be.
God never falters. The resistless tide
Of Temperance is sweeping grandly on,
In its majestic course; and very soon,
These old dead issues **of the war,** will sink
Bene t the slumb'ring shoreless, soundless Sea
Of deep Oblivion, to **rise no more.**

Already in the South—concerning this;
The most momentous question **of the age**—
Thefe is a mighty movement **breaking** forth:
For irrespective of past Party lines,
Our gifted, **noble** Southern Temp'rance men,
Are waiting anxiously, to clasp the **hands,**
Of Northern brethren, in this fearful fight,
Which shall at last, dethrone King Alcohol.
Shall **Northern men** reject these **out-stretched hands?**
No, **Never!** We are ready Brethren dear;

To meet with you "half way." Then let us leave
Our Rum-cursed Parties and together stand,
Beneath our Temp'rance banner, pure and white;
To battle side by side, with heart to heart,
In this, THE COMING CONFLICT of the age;
And soon we'll be, no longer twain but ONE.

Most rapidly, the South is sweeping past
The North, in this great Prohibition fight.
May it not be, that in return for what
We did to help them banish Slavery,
The South will teach us how to banish Rum?
It certainly begins to look that way.
The North and South alike must now divide
Not on the "Color," but the "Liquor" line.
The break was made in grand Atlanta's fight
Where White and Colored men pressed to the "Polls,"
Mixed up. Both races voting "wet and dry."
God grant that soon the North and South may know
No longer "Mason's, Dixon's line," but may divide
Along this line. "HOMES VERSUS VILE SALOONS."

We had an earnest, of what is to come;
Just lately, when our good and brave St. John
Of Kansas soil, and Maryland's noble son,
The honored William Daniel, joined their hands,
And pledged their lives; to Prohibition North;
To Prohibition South, and EVERYWHERE.

Oh, would we then be freed forevermore,
From this sad stigma, of a solid South
And North? Let statesman, politicians, all;
Each patriotic woman, man and child;
Each lover of his Country, and his God,
Forever cease from flaunting to the air
The "Bloody Shirt;" But let them everywhere,
O'er North and South, and East and West, unfurl

Blest Prohibition's banner to the breeze,
And soon—yes, very soon, a "SOLID SOUTH"
AND "SOLID NORTH" WILL BE NO MORE. "AMEN."

XXII.

Moreover Prohibition, WILL PROMOTE
OUR NATION'S HONOR; and before the eyes
Of other countries, classes, kindreds, climes,
Our grand old flag, the precious "stars and stripes,"
Will bear a glory, scarcely dreamed of now,
If only, this grand principle of Truth,
Is once emblazoned clearly on its folds.

If asked, "but how can this be done?" we say;
OUR NATION'S CONSTITUTION MUST BE CHANGED.
This document, which is our written law,
The honest, honored declaration of our will,
Is NOT YET PERFECT. When at first 'twas made,
It did not teach ALL governmental Truth
And could not; for some truths were then unknown
To most, if not to all our leading men
Of these truths, some are known; while others still
Remain to be disclosed, in future years.

Amendments have been—yea, and must be made,
If we would have our Constitution keep
Apace with progress, and with new-found Truth:
Some very foolishly object to these;
All such, declare, "we never have gone wrong,
But were PERFECTION, from the very first."
The object of our Constitution, is;
To fully, clearly speak the people's will,
Respecting all our National affairs.
On Earth, none is infallible, but God:
And hence, the People's will may not be right.

'Tis only when the People's will bespeaks
The holy will of God, that it can stand
The test of time.   No QUESTION EVER IS;
Or CAN BE SETTLED, TILL IT'S SETTLED RIGHT:
And that will always be, in God's own way,
And in accordance with His changeless Truth.

The World is getting better, age by age;
As one by one, the mighty conflicts waged,
Between the hosts of light, and fiends of Hell,
Are settled—yea, and settled for all time,
In favor of the hosts of Righteousness.

Our theory of Government, is based
Upon the doctrine, that the *People* rule;
That "WE THE PEOPLE, hold the sovereign right
To say, what shall, or what shall not be done."
'Tis true, that here, a sovereign People rule;
But whether we acknowledge it or not,
We rule, beneath the sovereign hand of Him,
" Who puts down one, and sets another up."
'Tis He who marshals men and nations too,
And as our Sovereign, bends our wills to His.
We are His people, and He uses us,
To fight for Him, against the hosts of sin.

To-day the Devil largely rules the World.
He and his hellish hosts, still hold their Fort:
This as his Citadel, is so well built,
That seemingly, no force could ever shake,
The firm foundations of its deep-laid walls,
Around this Fort, at certain distances,
He has erected, "Breast-Works" strong and high,
And planted mighty "Batteries," from which
This wily Leader of the fiends of Hell,
Has been for many ages, and is still,
Not only mowing down the ranks of man,
But keeping back the progress of the Truth.

The Sovereign Ruler of the Universe,
Has, once for all, decreed eternal war,
Against the Devil and his hellish hordes.
Their mighty Citadel must be destroyed;
These hosts of darkness, bound with endless chains,
And cast into that lake of brimstone fire,
Where they shall be tormented evermore.
But first, to reach the Devil's central Fort,
And by, at last, destroying it, obtain
The final victory; his "Breast-Works" must
Be taken, and his "Batteries" be stormed.
To this great work, our Sovereign Savior, King,
Our "Captain of Salvation" leads His hosts:
And one by one, these "Breast-Works" must go down:
And one by one, these mighty "Batteries"
Of sin and error, grief and woe, shall be
Forever silenced, by the arms of Truth.

We have been waging one of these great wars.
The smoke has scarcely cleared; the horrid din
Of battle scarcely ceased to wring our ears;
But this we know. The battle has been fought;
The vict'ry won; and *Slavery is dead*.
This "Breast-Work" has been taken; and its guns
Forever "spiked" in silence stand, except
As trophies of the triumph of the Truth.
Behold, our Monument of victory!
It stands imbedded in our Nation's law:
For by our Constitution, ALL ARE FREE
Whatever be their color or their race.

But shall we now rest satisfied with this?
Ah, No! Our enemies are not yet dead;
Although repulsed, they are not overcome.
Their crafty Leader (as his custom is,
When one ' breast-work" or "battery" is stormed;
But strengthens still more carefully the *next:*

That when the one is taken, he may find
Behind the other, safety from his foes)
Has only led his hosts of darkness back,
Behind a stronger wall, and seeks to wage,
With greater guns, and still more fiendish zeal,
A fiercer conflict with the hosts of Truth.

Behind what "Breast-work" now does Satan lurk?
What mighty "Batteries" are belching forth,
Hell's most destructive deadly volleys now ?
Look closely ! See ! upon that breast-work there,
In letters lurid with the glow of Hell,
These awful words. "RUM, WHISKY, BRANDY, GIN."
Look, look ! when for a moment, that dense smoke
Around those great grim guns, shall clear away !
Behold those guns! those death-inflicting, aye,
Those woe-producing, soul-destroying guns !
On each, God's hand has written, "WINE AND BEER."
How long shall our poor race, by millions die,
Shot down by these death-dealing guns of Rum ?
How long shall our whole World sit dumb with woe,
Nor lift a finger for its own relief,
From all this poverty, distress and death,
Brought on it, by its traffic in strong drink ?   .

Thank God! our weeping world is waking up.
Behold America ! "Land of the free;
Home of the brave" is leading forth her hosts !
Here, holy men of God, are pitting guns,
Grand, Prohibition, life-preserving guns,
Against the Devil's deadly batteries;
And by their votes, are pouring red-hot shot,
Into the breast-works of infernal Rum.
Already sev'ral breaches have been made.
In Kansas, and in Iowa and Maine,
The battle has been fought, a vict'ry won;
And through the ever-wid'ning breach thus made,

Still other States around them, **North** and **South**,
And East and West, are quickly pressing in.

To arms ! TO ARMS ! ! O Temp'rance Warriors ! Come !
Our Country, aye the World beseeches **us**,
To fight for "God and Home and Native **Land**."
Oh, let us never stop, until we place
Pure Prohibit.on, in our Nation's law,
And make our Constitution nobly say:
" HENCEFORTH NO MAN SHALL MANUFACTURE, SELL,
OR KEEP FOR SALE, IN THESE UNITED STATES
FOREVER, ANYTHING TO MAKE MEN DRUNK."

We have no sympathy **with Temp'rance men,**
Who in their wild extravagance, **assert**
That just so soon as Prohibition comes,
At once Millenial days will dawn on Earth,
Our sinful World become a Paradise."
The Prohibition of Strong Drink, of course,
Will prove a priceless boon to all our race,
And make our Earth, a far more happy home;
For Liquor Prohibition, means far more
Than death to **Rum.**   This does not stand alone.
The principle of Prohibition rests
In God's eternal Truth.   And we believe
That many Prohibitionists to-day
Are building **better,** wiser than they know,
Or even dream. **For** by stern Logic's law,
It follows, that if Nations have the right
To stop importing, making, selling Drink,
Beyond all doubt they have the right to stop
The importation, manufacture, sale,
Of EVERY OTHER noxious, hurtful drug.
Hence when "SALOONS SHALL GO," we soon **shall see**
Tobacco, Opium, and all such things
Close at their heels. *Most fit companionship!!!*
This answers those who constantly affirm,

" That Prohibitionists, expect to form
A new "Third Party" for most everything."

The Prohibition Party will fulfill
Its noble mission, then will soon become
Corrupt and DIE.   And though it will do much
To bless mankind, it will not banish sin,
Nor make a blissful Paradise of Earth.
For there are other woes besides Strong Drink
Which curse our World.   New Parties will arise
To grapple with, and put these evils down;
And as each Battle's fought, each vict'ry won,
Its grand results, will be forever clinched
Within the "Constitution" of the Land.

The "Sacred Number Seven" which denotes
The period of rest, we are inclined
To think, applies not only to "days, months
And years," but to "Millenniums" as well.
If our "Chronology" should be correct,
The Seven-Thousandth Period of Man
The blest "Millennial age" of Earth, will dawn
Within One Hundred years.   Hence we believe
About the close of the next Century
Will rise, "THE CHRISTIAN PARTY" to espouse
The principles of "National Reform."
Within this grandest Party of them all
None but true Christians shall obtain a place.
God's Name will be acknowledged, and His Word
Be made the basis of all human laws;
Against this Christian Party, will be massed
All wicked men, and all the fiends of Hell:
Earth's "Armageddon" battle will be fought.
Truth shall prevail.   Our Savior, Jesus Christ,
The rightful Ruler of the Universe,
Be crowned, "THE KING OF KINGS AND LORD OF LORDS."

But leaving "Speculation" this we know,
There is no Country under Heav'n, to-day;
Where this great COMING CONFLICT of the age,
Can be more quickly waged successfully:
For through God's goodness, in this land of ours;
Each man's a sovereign, and each man is free.
Between our shores and those of other lands,
Great Oceans roll; and so we do not need,
Vast standing armies, to maintain our rights.
Nor are our faces ground into the dust,
By those extravagant and heavy drains
Which must be levied on a Nation's wealth,
To feed the useless pomp of royal thrones,
With all their pampered Aristocracies.
For these and other reasons, in this fight
Against Intemperance, and all its woes;
We have the grandest prospect for success,
Of any other nation on the Globe.

Oh, if consistent with His holy will,
May God grant us this HONOR, to be first
Among the mighty Nations of the Earth,
To fling a Temp'rance BANNER to the winds,
And as a TEMP'RANCE NATION, BLESS THE WORLD,
For if our Country would "prohibit" Drink,
All other Nations soon would do the same.

Oh, Fellow-Countrymen ! let us improve
Our glorious opportunity to fight,
(Save that, by which, our Saviour vanquished Sin,)
The grandest battle Earth has ever seen.
We fight not for ourselves, but for the World.
The victory is hard to win; BUT SURE.
God grant us courage, patience, Faith; and soon
Flung from the mast-head of our "Ship of State,"
Our grand old "Stars and Stripes" shall kiss the skies,
And all (and none more proud than we) shall see

Emblazoned clearly, on its ample folds
There side by side, not only that grand Truth;
" ETERNAL ABOLITION, FROM THE SIN
Of SLAVERY" but that still grander Truth;
" ETERNAL PROHIBITION, FROM THE CURSE,
AND CRIME OF ALCOHOLIC DRUNKENNESS."

XXIII.

Another problem, will be largely solved,
If Prohibition shall become our law—
A problem, with which few can be compared,
As fraught with more momentous interests
Of pressing prominence, and magnitude,
To our own Land, as well as to the World.
THIS GIANT IMMIGRATION PROBLEM, stands,
And stares us in the face.   What shall we do ?
By thousands, emigrants from foreign lands,
Are flocking to our shores, to find a home.
From every Country, and from every clime
They come; and never in our history,
Has this, our highly favored land, received
So vast an influx, from across the seas,
As in the last few years.   An army comes
Each year, at least, FIVE HUNDRED THOUSAND STRONG.
Our Country's flooded now, and *still they come.*

But what effect, will all these hosts produce,
Upon our Country ?   Surely such a mass
Of human-kind, *a half a million souls,*
Thus poured upon us, year by year, must have
No SMALL EFFECT, UPON OUR NATION'S LIFE.
Whence do these foreign thousands chiefly come?
We answer.   Largely from the Rum-cursed lands
Of Europe.   And they bring along with them,
Their social drinking habits; and expect

To exercise the same sweet liberty (?)
And to enjoy the same sweet (?) customs, here
With us, they loved so well, beyond the seas.

How can we hope, that those who have been taught,
From early baby-hood, to look upon
Intoxicating drinks, just as they would,
The every-day necessities of life,
To help our grand, good Temp'rance cause along?
They *don't* do it; and what is worse, they *won't*
Do it. The great majority of them,
Are bitterly opposed, to Temp'rance work,
And Temp'rance laws. Ten thousands of them come
And with a little money of their own,
Or with a little borrowed from their friends;
They buy some whisky, and a keg of beer—
Put out their signs; and soon build up a trade.
Quite frequently the *man* goes out to work.
The *woman* keeps the shop; and as they live
On nothing nearly—soon we find them *rich.*
How do they use their beer and whisky wealth?
Do all these foreign Liquor-Dealers seek,
To keep INTEMP'RANCE out of Politics?
By no means. Everywhere they clamor long
And loud—"Let all these silly Temp'rance laws,
And Sunday laws, be speedily repealed:
We came here to be free (?) Nor will we have
Our liberties (?) in anywise curtailed."
Their aim is to transform America,
Ere-long, into a grand *fac-simile,*
Of their own happy (?) glorious Father-land.

All must admit. They have succeeded well.
Go, visit any City in our Land;
And you will find "Beer-Gardens" everywhere,
So like those seen across the rolling deep;
That if you did not know, in other ways—

Than by inspecting these beer-guzzling hells—
You could not tell, upon which Continent
You stood. Beer-burdened Europe, or our own
Beer-cursed United States? *But worst of all;*
Our Politicians, heed the siren song,
Of those engaged in this infernal trade,
And stand entranced. With shame, we must confess;
That foreign Liquor-Dealers largely hold
Our Government, in their own hands to-day,
And can and DO dictate to us, what line
Of policy, we must henceforth pursue.

This Country (though we may not know it) is,
Bound down beneath the iron hand of Rum,
And lorded over, by the "Liquor Ring"
A large per-cent. of which, comes from abroad.
See, how our politicians, bow and scrape,
In blind submission to this foreign vote;
Nor do they ever dare to stem its tide.
How long, O Countrymen ! shall things thus be ?
How long, shall these vile men, not only rule,
But *ruin*, this fair land, which welcomes them
With open arms, to come and occupy
Its fertile fields, and share its happy homes ?

For, one long century, and more, we have
Conducted our National affairs,
Untrammeled by dictation from afar:
And independently of other lands,
Have sailed our "Ship of State" to suit ourselves:
And shall we now submit to those whose tastes,
And habits, have been formed in other climes,
And under circumstances so diverse
From ours here? And shall we let them come,
And guide in their own way, our "Ship of State ?"
No ! no ! ! we'll still cling firmly to the helm;
And by God's grace, we will in His good time,

Eternally prohibit from **our Land,**
This whole infernal traffic in strong **drink,**
In spite of every Foreigner on Earth,
Who **dares to** undertake to stop our work.
And if our foreign brethren do not like,
This wholesale Prohibition of Drink's curse;
They are at perfect liberty to go,
Back to those Rum-cursed countries, whence they cam

Thank God ! ALL FOREIGNERS are NOT the *friends,*
Of this detestable and dreadful trade.
Some of the **best** and **noblest** Temp'rance men
And women, that have ever trod our soil,
Have come to us from lands **across the seas.**
(From their **fair brows** no laurels **would we pluck.**)
While this is true; the great sad fact **remains:**
That for one Temp'rance man, who comes to us
From foreign lands; there are perhaps **a** score,
Who drink intoxicants; and what is worse,
Expect **to make a** living, **by their sale.**
'Tis said, **to be** a fact beyond **all doubt;**
That in our land t -day, there are more men
And women, dea'ii g **out** eternal **death**
Through Drink, of foreign than **of native** birth.
These liquor-dealing hosts, are mighty now,
And constantly grow stronger, day by day,
As foreign countries **land** their liquor hordes,
Upon **our shores by** thousands, **to** augment
The rapidly increasing **might of** Rum.
What shall **we do?** We are almost controlled
Already, by **these** foreign liquor-vending Lords:
If something is not **done,** 'twill not be long,
Till they shall bind **our Nation,** hand and foot,
The helpless **slaves of Bacchus.** No, THEY'LL NOT.
THERE IS A JUST AND HOLY GOD ON HIGH.

Awake, Americans ! All Temp'rance men
Of native, and of foreign birth ! **Arise** !

And, stem this tide, while it can be controlled !
Oh, let us seize this Monster by the horns,
And pour hot Prohibition down his throat
Until he dies.   Let us still hold the helm;
And tell our foreign brethren, "If they come
To dwell with us, *they must leave Rum behind,*"
When this is nobly, kindly, firmly done;
THE IMMIGRATION PROBLEM WILL BE SOLVED.

We would not turn away a single soul,
Who seeks a happy home in our free Land.
To worthy, homeless brethren, everywhere,
In other climes, and other lands, we say;
' Come thou with us, and we will do thee good."
Most welcome ! yes, *thrice welcome* to our shores !
Our fields and forests: all our treasured mines;
Our almost countless prairies, rich and broad;
Our mountains and our hills; Our rivers, lakes;
Our hamlets, towns and cities; *all are free—*
Free as the air we breathe—to those who wish,
To be henceforward, true Americans.
Hence to our brother Emigrants, we say;
" We welcome you; but when you come, you must
Become Americans.   You must submit
To Temp'rance, and all other righteous laws."
" On these conditions, gladly, to our homes;
Our hospitality, our happiness;
We welcome you: But never shall you sweep
Away, our Sabbath and our Temp'rance laws,
More dear to Christian men, than life itself."
Once more, we welcome you; but this we say;
" *You can not Germanize America.*"

God grant us Prohibition, and our Land
Already greatly favored from on High,
Would soon become, what it now boasts to be;
A grand Asylum for all those distressed,

Oppressed, down-trodden millions of our race,
Who never can own homes in foreign lands;
But who, beneath our Prohibition flag,
Could find a happiness, elsewhere unknown.
God grant ! that soon this flag may be unfurled !
Then we'll not fear these floods, from foreign lands,
But gladly bid them welcome, to our shores,
Till every nook of this—our vast Domain,
Shall be filled up, with happy Christian Homes.
Then in Longfellow's deathless-words, we'll cry,

" Thou too, sail on, O Ship of State,
Sail on, O Union, strong and great.
Humanity with all its fears,
With all its hopes of future years,
Is hanging breathless on thy fate.

* * * * * * *

Sail on, nor fear to breast the sea,
Our hearts, our hopes, are all with thee.
Our hearts, our hopes, our prayers, our tears,
Our faith triumphant o'er our fears,
Are all with Thee.   Are all with Thee."

XXIV.

There is no doubt, that Prohibition would,
PROVE AN INCALCULABLY PRECIOUS BOON
To WOMAN: weak to helplessness, perhaps,
In point of physical ability.
When brought in conflict with the strength of man;
But strong, aye more, well nigh invincible,
In everything that's noble, good and true.
She can not take the sword, and *fight* her way
To victory.   But she can take her heart,
And pour it out in prayer, before her God;
" And will He not avenge His own elect,

Although He bear long " with her enemies?
HER GREATEST ENEMY, TO-DAY, IS RUM.

Who suffers most from this vile Demon Drink?
Who reaps the foulest and most bitter fruits,
From this great crime, of which she often is,
As innocent as are those holy hosts
Of Angels, praising God around His throne ?
Who sits, and waits, and weeps, through sleepless nights,
It may be, by the ragged cot, which holds
Her starving, dying babe; and list'ning seeks,
(Through all those blinding, bitter tears, which seem,
Almost to blister her poor pallid cheeks,)
To hear the halting, swagg'ring step of him,
Who *once* was tender, noble, kind and true,
But now, Alas ! through Drink, a *very Fiend ?*
Oh 'tis the drunken husband's wretched wife,
Who sits and weeps, in weary watchfulness,
And wishes he would come; although she knows
Full well, that always, when he does reel home;
Each echo of that drunken step will strike
Dread horror, to her soul.   And thus she lives,

          A true, pure wife,
          Mid hopes and fears,
          Mid prayers and tears,
          A dreadful life:

          Until in love,
          God gives her rest,
          Amid the blest,
          In realms above.

Talk not of "individual liberty !"
What individual freedom, has that wife
Whose heart is broken, by her husband's Rum?
What mother has such Liberty, who dies,

Beneath the stroke of some besotted son?
What drunkard's daughter, sister, anywhere,
Can boast of liberty for life or limb,
So long as "father" or as "brother" drinks?

Oh, give us Prohibition, and at once,
'Twill free these noble women from that curse,
Which now so often, binds them, hand and foot,
Beneath a **Slavery**, far **worse** than death;
Or quickly crushes them into the grave.
Oh, noble Godly women! "Fear ye not,
Nor be dismayed." **For you** a brighter day
Is surely dawning. By your holy hands
Uplifted **to** the skies; King Alcohol
Must die. Think you, that **all those prayers and** tears,
Of your "CRUSADE" were unavailing? NO!
Ten million voices answer. No! *No!!* No!!!
Each "tear is bottled" and each earnest prayer,
Is ringing **in the ears of Him, who** guides
The worlds, and holds in check, the fiends of Hell;
And yet, whose gracious ear is ever bent,
To hear and heed, the humblest, faintest cry
Of every child of Heav'n. This GRAND "CRUSADE,"
Of noble, holy, Christian WOMAN-HOOD,
Against the "most gigantic crime of crimes"—
The most colossal evil ever known,
Since Satan first seduced our race to sin—
Was but the dawning of that blessed day,
When Prohibition's flag shall float on high,
O'er every Country, and o'er every Sea:
Then none will kiss its folds, with more delight,
Than those poor women who have felt the sting,
Of that vile monstrous Demon of Strong-Drink.

It was a woman, linked our Earth to God,
By bringing forth His "Well-Beloved Son!
And when He died; it was a woman stood

Last at the cross: and when He rose again,
It was a woman, who first worshiped Him:
It was a woman, sent Columbus forth,
To find the wonders of a Western World:
It was a woman, wrote that wondrous book,
Which largely, struck the shackles from the slave,
And set four million human beings free:
It was our noble women, who began
This grand Crusade against accursed Drink.
These precious women, full of faith in God,
And full of love for all poor drunken ones,
Have joined their hearts, in agonizing prayer,
For grace to overthrow the curse of Rum;
And taking for their motto, "God and Home,
And Native Land," they've grown so strong, that now,
Next to the blessed Church of Jesus Christ,
The " Woman's Christian Temp'rance Union " stands
The most determined and efficient foe,
Against Strong Drink, the world has ever seen;
And through its power, at no distant day,
This whole vile traffic shall go down to death.

Oft in counting human greatness,
  And in reck'ning noble deeds,
Woman's work has been forgotten,
  As God's holy cause she pleads;

But as man becomes more perfect,
  And Truth's banner is unfurled,
All must say, " The hand of Woman
  Is the hand that moves the world."

XXV.

And lastly, but by far the best of all,
This precious Prohibition will promote
The cause of Christ. And here, at least, we can

Appeal to every lover of the Cross,
To every true disciple of the Lamb.

There's nothing in the world which so impedes
The Gospel's onward, upward march, to-day,
As does this liquor traffic's hell-wrought curse.
The Devil hold's no weapon in his hands
At once more deadly, more effective, than
This mighty, monstrous power of Strong Drink.
Let heralds of the Cross go where they may
To bear " good tidings of great joy " to men,
And they will always find the Demon Drink
Stretched out in fiendish glee across their path.
It is no wonder Christian ministers,
And other Christian workers, oft become
Disheartened, when they see, on every hand,
These foul, accursed dram shops growing up
Around them and undoing their good work
More rapidly than they can get it done.
No wonder, in the sadness of their hearts,
They often cry, " How long, oh Lord, how long,
Shall Satan's forces plot against the Lord
And His Anointed, saying: Let us break
Their bands and cast away their cords from us ? "

The Church is languishing beneath a cloud.
From every congregation in the land,
From all denominations comes this cry,
" Oh, for more life and light!" Whence comes this cloud ?
Whence springs this longing cry for light and life ?
Is God not able to revive His Church ?
Why then this darkness and this cry ? Hear now,
Ye chosen children of the Living God!
Does he not plainly say, " If ye indeed
Regard iniquity within your hearts
I will not hear ? " He hears us not, because
Vast numbers who profess the name of Christ

Are open partners in this liquor crime.
And can we hope that God will ever pour
His Spirit out upon us, or revive
His work within our hearts, till from our feet
We shake the dust of this vile Demon Drink,
And for all time hurl from our poor, galled necks,
The dread dominion of his cruel yoke?

Just think of it.   For more than fifty years
God's people have been voting whisky straight,
Without a "scratch."   Unconsciously, 'tis true,
But none the less effectively.   How can
We any longer wonder that the Church
Should languish unrevived, and call in vain
For fresh baptisms of the Holy Ghost?
Our monstrous, giant sin, of unsuppressed,
And unprohibited Intemperance,
Has gone up like a thick black cloud; and hides,
Behind its density, our Father's face.

Before we cast the first opposing stone,
Against the drunkard, and these Liquor men ;
Oh, let us stop, and as true Christians, ask,
" Are WE entirely free from sin OURSELVES
In this respect?"   Oh, let us ever strive,
To exercise, true Christian charity,
And ask ourselves, if our own skirts
Are clear; before denouncing all who drink,
Or sell strong drink, as murderers and knaves.
By helping "license" this vile traffic's wrongs,
Have WE not been upholding this foul trade ?
And have we not been going to the polls
Year·after year, and standing side by side,
With liquor-dealing knaves, of every sort,
Been casting in our ballots, just like theirs—
The votes of Doctors of Divinity,

Identical, in all respects, with those
Cast by the Keepers of the worst saloons?

Perhaps (?) there are a few true, honest men,
Engaged in this dread drunkard trade. *They're wrong;*
Yes, WRONG MOST TERRIBLY: and yet the blame
Should not ALL rest on Liquor men alone.
No! NO!! *The Church is to a great extent
Responsible, for this dire, deadly Curse.*
How long would Strong Drink, triumph over Truth
And Temperance, if all the Christian men
And women, in this so-called Christian Land,
Would come out and oppose it? NOT TEN YEARS.

The Church must change. She must forever cease
Her whisky voting, and "come up to help
The Lord against the mighty." Old and young;
And rich and poor: let every Christian man;
Let all our Christian women, everywhere;
Let Christian boys and girls, all seize their swords,
And fight this COMING CONFLICT of our age.
For Prohibition, let all Christians **pray**:
For Prohibition, let us speak and work;
For Prohibition, let us always vote,
And Prohibition, soon will come to stay.

Quite often, you will hear the statement made;
" If Christians would let Prohibition be,
And not be foolish and fanatical,
And drag this Question into Politics;
But go to work, converting Liquor men,
Then we would need no Temp'rance laws at all,
To banish Rum. You can not *legislate
Morality into the human race;*
'Tis **vain to** try to make men good by law."
Perhaps we can't. But we *can* legislate
Great Immoralities **away from men.**

We can, BY LAW, shut up these vile Saloons,
And thus remove, temptations from the paths,
Of many millions of our rum-cursed race,
Who otherwise would fill the Drunkard's grave.
Our Government forbids the sale of Drink
To Indians and to Criminals. Why can't
We have some Legislation FOR OUR HOMES ?

To those who tell us, "we should go to work
Converting Liquor men," we humbly ask:
How CAN WE REACH these poor deluded ones ?
They will not come to Church, and if we go
To their Saloons; and talk to them of Christ,
And tell the story of His wondrous Love;
We would get only curses in return;
Perhaps (if we persisted) something worse.

How can we ever lead men to espouse
The cause of Christ, whose bodies and whose brains
Are steeped in beer and brandy; and still worse,
Whose consciences are stifled by their greed
For gold, and hellish thirst for gain ? Besides,
None can convert a soul but God alone.
" Paul plants. Apollos waters; but 'tis God
Who gives the increase." Now will God go down,
Into these vile saloons, and liquor dens,
And work a most stupendous miracle—
Converting all these drunkards, and these still
More loathsome Liquor-Dealers; while vast hosts,
Of His own children, pat them on the back,
And by their whisky votes, most plainly say;
" Go on ! Oh, Liquor-Dealers ! we will see,
That you are well protected in your work ? "
Our God will work no such a miracle;
But in His own good time, will open wide
The eyes of these His children, and will show
Them, what they have been doing all these years:

Then they will find, to their astonishment,
That all this time, they have been voting Rum,
And thus have fostered, their most deadly foe.

God has already opened many eyes:
For in our late Election's stormy fight,
An host, well-nigh THREE-HUNDRED THOUSAND STRONG,
Stood up for Prohibition and the Right,
And by their votes spoke out for God and Truth.
'Tis true, we could not now elect our men,
Yet we have shown to all our growing strength,
And soon ALL CHRISTIAN men will join our ranks,
And under Prohibition's Banner stand,
And as one man, lift up their hearts to God,
For grace, to "pulverize the Demon Drink."
Then, not till then, will that dark cloud, which now,
Rests like a pall, upon the Church of Christ,
Be lifted from between us and our God:
Then, not till then, will "Zion rise and shine;
The glory of her God beam o'er her work;"
Then, not till then will great Revivals come,
To cheer the weary Heralds of the Cross.

Oh, Fellow-Christians ! Whence those precious days,
Of Eighteen-Fifty-Seven, Eight and Nine?
It was because, in Eighteen-Fifty-Six,
Vast numbers of God's children, dared do right,
And nobly took their stand, upon God's side,
Against the awful Curse of Slavery.
If we may judge the future, by the past;
Then may we well believe, that just as soon,
As God's own people, all united stand
With Him, against this even greater Curse
Than Slavery—this horrid Liquor Crime—
That just so soon, but not before, will God
Throw open wide, the windows of His grace,
And "pour us out a blessing, till we shall

Not have room to receive." Then shall we have
Such grand "Revival Times" throughout our Land,
As never have been known on Earth, before.
Then by ten thousands (when their shops are closed)
These Liquor men, will turn unto the Lord:
And as a token, that they are sincere
In their Conversion; they will gladly take
Much of the blood-stained gold, which they had gained
By selling Drink, and lay it at Christ's feet,
To send His Gospel, to those heathen lands,
Where countless millions, now go down to death,
Without the knowledge, of the Way of Life

Our Land will then no longer send, as now;
Stores of "New England Rum" down in the holds,
Of those same ships, which bear the men of God,
To heathen lands, there, to undo their work,
And blast their brightest hopes of doing good;
Until these Missionaries of the cross,
Beholding ruin wrought, on every hand,
(Whole heathen nations, drunk with Christian (?) Rum!!)
Lift up their voices, in their deep despair,
And cry back to their Country: "Stop! Oh, STOP!!
For these poor heathens' sake, STOP SENDING RUM!"

Well might our Christian (?) Country, hide her head,
And blush with shame; to think that HEATHEN LANDS,
Still plead with her, in vain, to stop this trade.
In view of this one fact, how can a man—
A Christian man, vote longer for Strong Drink?
Thank God! these heathen cries are not in vain.
God reigns. The cup of Drink, is almost full.
Our happy Earth, shall soon prohibit Rum.

Oh! Christian Toiler? let this cheer your heart,
And for this object, ever humbly pray:
Oh, plant your Prohibition Banner, firm,

In every valley; **On each** mountain top;
Unfurl its folds, in every breeze that blows
On land or **sea.** Then blessed be our **God!!**
The countless millions, **of** accursed Rum,
Instead of bringing woe, will soon be turned,
Into the blessed service, of our God;
To clothe the naked: Feed the poor:
To comfort, civilize, and CHRISTIANIZE THE WORLD.

Awake! Oh, Voice of Truth! Awake! Arise!
Let Prohibition ring throughout our skies;
Then shall we all, with boundless joy, rejoice,
Exclaiming, with one, universal voice;
" We've slain this Monster of our Sin **and** Shame,
And swept his stigma, from our Nation's **name.**"

May God in mercy, speed that happy day,
When this great evil, shall have passed away.
Then Love, and Joy, and Peace, will all unite,
To make and keep, each Home's pure hearth-stone bright

XXVI.

Now, **in** CONCLUSION, let this word **be said:**
The victory is ours. *This we know.*
FOR PROHIBITION'S RIGHT, AND WILL PREVAIL.
It has been wisely said, "Truth crushed to Earth,
Shall rise again: God's endless years, are hers."
This Prohibition Cause, has been assailed,
Both by pretended friends, and bitter foes,
Time and again; until she sometimes seemed,
To be almost, if not completely crushed:
But God has raised her up; and now we see,
The lips of triumph, pressed against **her** cheek,
And hear on every hand the **happy** shout,
Her time has come. Her victory is near.
She has been **crushed.** She never shall be, more.

A half a million men, who deal out death
And woe, to fifty millions, of their race,
Can not much longer, hold complete control,
Against ten millions of free men, whose votes
Shall soon lay low, the deadly Demon Drink.
Some point us to our little Party vote,
And ask us, "What can such a vote affect?"
And others, sneering at us, call us fools,
And say, "We only throw away our votes."
What did the votes for James G. Birney do?
Were Fremont votes, all "thrown away?" Ah, no!
A VOTE FOR PRINCIPLE IS NEVER LOST.
A vote for God can not be thrown away,
But stands, a constant witness to His Truth,
And soon will multiply a thousand fold.

In Eighteen-Forty, James G. Birney polled,
A little over seven thousand votes:
Two decades after, Abra'm Lincoln went
Into the "White House" as our President.

Look at our Prohibition vote, to-day.
See how its grown, in spite of scoffs and sneers.
Our Leaders, may be burnt in effigy,
Or in reality, for aught we know (?)
Our noble "Haddocks" murdered in cold blood;
But God will raise up others, in their stead,
To fight the battles of His precious Truth,
Until, at last the victory is won.

Oh, Prohibition Warriors! "Form in line!!"
Already this grand battle has begun.
The States of Iowa, and Kansas, both
Are pressing on: While grand, old Maine still stands,
Firm in the fore-front, of the raging strife·
Clad in her armor, all invincible,
She fights for Prohibition; cheering on

Her sister States, to follow in her steps,
And smite this Liquor Traffic, till it dies.

But Prohibitionists ! Be not deceived:
We wage this war against a *mighty foe.*
The liquor interests, are deep and broad,
And they are fighting for their very life.
These Liquor men are energetic, shrewd,
Determined, men of minds and men of means;
Besides, they are completely organized;
For, bound together by their horrid oaths
And still more horrid traffic, as ONE MAN
They stand united to oppose the hosts
Of Prohibition battling for their God
And for their homes and for HUMANITY.
But mighty as the hosts of Rum may be,
THEY MUST GO DOWN before the onward march
Of Justice, Mercy, Righteousness, and Truth.
The victory will come. Yes! YES! 'TWILL COME,
As truly as there is a God on high
Who sees the tears and hears the bitter cries
Of his poor, Rum-cursed children.
                                    We appeal
To **every citizen,** especially
To every CHRISTIAN citizen, in these
United States, to pray and work and VOTE
For PROHIBITION, TILL ITS TRIUMPH COMES
AND THIS DREAD LIQUOR TRAFFIC IS DESTROYED.

We ask it in the name of Christ our Lord,
And in the name of all that's holy, just,
And good, and true. We ask it in the name
Of all these billions, of our Nation's wealth,
Now worse than wasted, through this horrid trade:
We ask it in the name, of working men,
Whose lives are cursed, by this infernal Drink:
We ask it in the name, of beggared Homes;

Of weeping, wretched, Mothers, Sisters, Wives,
And starving, ragged children: In the name,
Of our poor drunkards; yea, and in the name,
Of blinded Liquor Dealers; In the name,
Of colleges and schools: and in the name,
Of those grand principles, which shall secure,
Our Nation's peace, and perpetuity:
Aye more, we ask it in the name, of HOPE
AND HAPPINESS AND HEAV'N; OH! NEVER CAST
ANOTHER BALLOT, FOR THE FIERY FIEND
OF RUM: No! NEVER! NEVER!! NEVERMORE!!!

May that Infinite and Eternal One,
Who taught us, Prohibition, is His will—
The greatest Revolution of the age—
The greatest step of progress, man has made,
Toward that glad time, when all Earth's, "Kingdoms shall
Become the kingdoms of our Lord and Christ".—
May that Infinite and Eternal One,
Help every one of us, to be henceforth,
True to ourselves, and to our Loved Ones, true;
True to our Country, and HUMANITY,
AND LAST AND BEST OF ALL, TRUE TO OUR GOD.

The End.

www.ingramcontent.com/pod-product-compliance
Lightning Source LLC
Chambersburg PA
CBHW030602270326
41927CB00007B/1022